LEGENDS OF WARFARE
NAVAL

USS Enterprise (CV-6)

The "Big E" from the Doolittle Raid, Midway & Santa Cruz to Guadalcanal & Leyte

DAVID DOYLE

SCHIFFER MILITARY

4880 Lower Valley Road • Atglen, PA 19310

Designed by Justin Watkinson
Type set in Impact/Minion Pro/Univers LT Std

ISBN: 978-0-7643-6075-6
Printed in China

Published by Schiffer Publishing, Ltd.
4880 Lower Valley Road
Atglen, PA 19310
Phone: (610) 593-1777; Fax: (610) 593-2002
E-mail: Info@schifferbooks.com
www.schifferbooks.com

For our complete selection of fine books on this and related subjects, please visit our website at www.schifferbooks.com. You may also write for a free catalog.

Schiffer Publishing's titles are available at special discounts for bulk purchases for sales promotions or premiums. Special editions, including personalized covers, corporate imprints, and excerpts, can be created in large quantities for special needs. For more information, contact the publisher.

We are always looking for people to write books on new and related subjects. If you have an idea for a book, please contact us at proposals@schifferbooks.com.

Acknowledgments

In compiling this history I was truly blessed to have the invaluable help of many colleagues whom I am fortunate to call my friends, including Tracy White, James Noblin, Roger Torgeson, David Baker, and Dana Bell. Their generous and skillful assistance adds immensely to the quality of this volume. I am fortunate to include a unique collection of photos taken by Lt. Col. Herbert Alan Belin, which were generously provided by Michael-Ann Belin. I am especially blessed to have the ongoing help of my wonderful wife, Denise, who has scanned thousands of photos and documents for this and numerous other books. Beyond that, she has been an ongoing source of support and inspiration.

All photos are from the collections of the US National Archives and Records Administration unless otherwise noted.

Contents

Introduction   004

CHAPTER 1   Design and Construction   006

CHAPTER 2   Prelude to War   022

CHAPTER 3   Off to War   032

CHAPTER 4   Doolittle, Midway, and Tulagi   042

CHAPTER 5   Eastern Solomons, Santa Cruz, Naval Battle of Guadalcanal   054

CHAPTER 6   January 1943–June 1944   086

CHAPTER 7   July 1944–September 1945   102

CHAPTER 8   Navy Day, Magic Carpet, and the End of the "Big E"   122

Introduction

The US Navy's first carrier, the USS *Langley*, can be regarded as an experiment. Converted from the fleet collier USS *Jupiter*, this conversion was authorized on July 11, 1919, and was carried out by the Norfolk Navy Yard. The ship was recommissioned as the 14,000-ton USS *Langley*, CV-1, on March 30, 1922. Having proven that aircraft could be successfully launched, landed, and serviced from a specialized vessel, the way was paved for the next two carriers to join the US fleet—the *Lexington* (CV-2) and *Saratoga* (CV-3). Construction of both of these ships, intended to be the Navy's largest battle cruisers, had begun when the Washington Naval Treaty forbade their completion as such. It was permitted, however, that their hulls be utilized for the construction of two large aircraft carriers, displacing over 47,000 tons when fully loaded.

Even before *Lexington* and *Saratoga* entered service, plans were being drawn for the US Navy's first purpose-built aircraft carrier, which ultimately would be named USS *Ranger* (CV-4). With the treaty-imposed limitation of 69,000 remaining tons for aircraft carriers, the decision was made to build *Ranger* as a small carrier (as compared to *Lexington* and *Saratoga*), in an effort to be able to build a total of five vessels of such a size. At the time

construction of *Ranger* began, the US Navy had only a couple of years' experience operating the battle-ready carriers *Lexington* and *Saratoga*, so many of *Ranger*'s characteristics were instead based on experiences with the experimental *Langley*.

When serious consideration began to be given to the Navy's next generation of aircraft carriers in 1931, little had changed. Fortunately, by the time the actual order was placed in August 1933, the lessons taught by *Lexington* and *Saratoga* influenced the design.

The new ships would be 5,000 tons heavier and almost 100 feet longer than *Ranger*, include a power plant with twice the output, and be considerably better protected. While the new design was sound, unfortunately for the Navy there were no funds available to build the desired ships. That funding would not be available until 1933 and came from an unusual source—the National Industrial Recovery Act. This act, a key part of Franklin D. Roosevelt's "New Deal," included provisions for building thirty-two ships, including two aircraft carriers. The act was passed on June 16, 1933.

CV-3 *Saratoga* (*foreground*) and
CV-2 *Lexington* (*background*),
which had been converted to
aircraft carriers from the
incomplete hulls of battle
cruisers baring the same
names, were the nation's first
combat-ready aircraft carriers.
The two ships, which
comprised the Lexington-class,
joined the fleet in 1927.

Commissioned in 1934, CV-4
Ranger was the first United
States aircraft carrier to be
built from the keel up as such.
At 15,000 tons she was
substantially smaller than the
36,000-ton *Lexingtons*, an effort
to get more ships within the
limitations of the Washington
Treaty. Experience gained with
Ranger, as well as the
Lexingtons, was incorporated in
the Yorktown-class.

CHAPTER 1
Design and Construction

The Navy immediately solicited bids for the construction of the carriers and ultimately contracted with Newport News Shipbuilding and Dry Dock Company to build the ships, CV-5 and CV-6, on August 5, 1933. Just over a month later, the names of the vessels were chosen: CV-5 would be *Yorktown*, and CV-6 *Enterprise*.

Even though considerable planning had been done before the construction contract was issued, those plans evolved even after the contract was awarded. The flight deck was lengthened from the originally proposed 708 feet, going through several iterations before 816 feet was finally settled on, which was the flight deck length that ultimately was built. Similarly, the location and type of antiaircraft battery were revised.

The keel of *Enterprise* was laid down on Monday, July 16, 1934, about six weeks after that of the *Yorktown*. The two aircraft carriers rose from adjacent building ways in Virginia, considerably more alike than most sister ships of their size in that era.

Just under 116 weeks after the keel was laid, on Saturday, October 3, 1936, Mrs. Lulie H. Swanson, wife of Secretary of the Navy Claude A. Swanson, smashed a bottle of champagne against the hull near the forefoot, formally christening the vessel *Enterprise*.

That name, which had been approved by the secretary of the navy before the keel was laid, was recommended by RAdm. Ernest J. King, chief of the Bureau of Aeronautics (BuAer). In his August 11, 1933, recommendation, King wrote:

> This is one of the most famous names of the Navy through its association in the French, Revolutionary and Tripolitan wars. It dates back to the Revolutionary War, when it was borne by one of [Benedict] Arnold's vessels on Lake Champlain and later by a packet in the continental service on the Atlantic.

RAdm. William D. Leahy, chief of the Bureau of Navigation (BuNav), endorsed the selection of the name *Enterprise* on September 27, 1934: "to perpetuate the name borne" by the previous "fighting vessels of the United States Navy" named *Enterprise,* little knowing how much aircraft carrier number "6" would further distinguish the name.

Although afloat in Chesapeake Bay, *Enterprise* was far from being a complete warship. Thousands of tons of material, including miles of wiring and plumbing, guns, motors, ovens, and a myriad of other parts, had to be added in a process known as "fitting out" before *Enterprise* would transform from a hull to a ship.

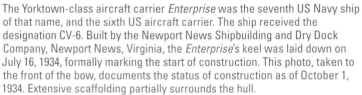

The Yorktown-class aircraft carrier *Enterprise* was the seventh US Navy ship of that name, and the sixth US aircraft carrier. The ship received the designation CV-6. Built by the Newport News Shipbuilding and Dry Dock Company, Newport News, Virginia, the *Enterprise*'s keel was laid down on July 16, 1934, formally marking the start of construction. This photo, taken to the front of the bow, documents the status of construction as of October 1, 1934. Extensive scaffolding partially surrounds the hull.

On the same date as the preceding photo, this view was taken from aft of the hull of the *Enterprise*, facing forward. As the bottom of the hull is built up, lateral frames are constructed, with plates of the shell, or outer skin of the hull, being riveted to the frames. These frames were assigned numbers, fore to aft, which would serve as constant references to specific locations on the longitudinal axis of the hull.

The *Enterprise* (*left*), and its sister ship and namesake of their carrier class, the *Yorktown* (CV-5) (*right*), are under construction, side by side, at Newport News Shipbuilding and Dry Dock on December 8, 1934. They are viewed from astern. These two carriers, along with the *Hornet* (CV-8), composed the Yorktown-class. The photo was taken from an aircraft assigned to the carrier USS *Ranger* (CV-4).

Enterprise, the hull on the upper ways, and *Yorktown*, lower, are viewed from above during construction on December 8, 1934. Construction was somewhat more advanced on the *Yorktown*; it was laid down two months before *Enterprise* and would be launched six months before *Enterprise*.

On April 2, 1935, almost nine months after the keel of the *Enterprise* was laid down, the progress of construction is shown in a photo taken from astern. In the foreground is the deck of the steering-gear room on the first platform (a platform being similar to a deck, but which does not extend the entire length of the hull). Note the double-bottomed construction of this feature, with the shell visible below the deck. The prominent hole in the floor is for the rudder shaft. Farther forward is a watertight, lateral bulkhead of special-treatment steel, to the front of which are bomb and ammunition storage spaces and the machinery spaces.

Work proceeds on the *Enterprise* on July 2, 1935, in a view taken from above the stern. The narrow section of deck in the foreground is very likely part of the fourth deck, as indicated by the presence of the rectangular trunk with scaffolding planks around it. Farther forward, construction of the third deck is well underway, and some of the framing for the second deck is present amidships. The second deck would be one level below the hangar deck.

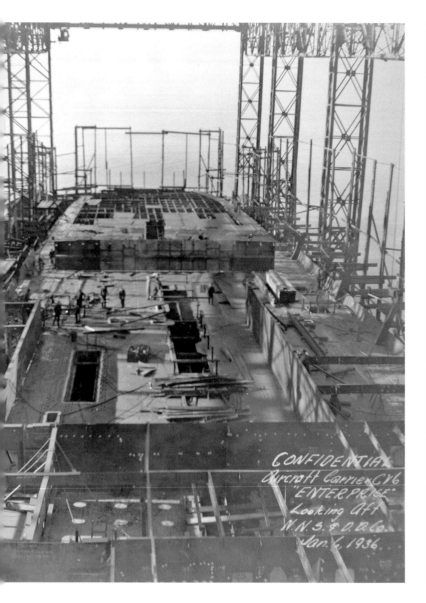

Work continued apace on the *Enterprise* on January 6, 1936, as seen in a photo above amidships facing aft.

The *Enterprise* presents its bow to the photographer on April 1, 1936. The upper level appears to be the hangar deck, also referred to as the main deck.

In another April 1, 1936, view of the *Enterprise*, the vantage point is above the aft part of the ship, facing forward, and again the upper level appears to be the hangar deck, with the aft elevator well in the foreground. Amidships is the center elevator well, which was offset to the starboard side of the centerline of the ship.

CONFIDENTIAL
Aircraft Carrier CV
"Enterprise"
Looking Forward
N.N.S.&D.D.Co.
April 1 1936

CONFIDENTIAL
AIRCRAFT CARRIER CV6
"ENTERPRISE"

As seen from above the aft end of the flight deck on October 1, 1936, the island, as the superstructure was called, on the starboard side of the flight deck is under construction, with scaffolding around it. In the foreground is the aft elevator, with a stovepipe jutting through an opening in it.

CONFIDENTIAL
Aircraft Carrier CV6
"ENTERPRISE"
Port Side
N.N.S. & D.D.Co.
Oct. 1, 1936.

The *Enterprise* is seen from off its port bow on the building ways on October 1, 1936, two days before its launching. The nameplate "ENTERPRISE" is visible below the edge of the forecastle deck, above and aft of the hawsepipe for the port anchor. The port anchor is secured to the side of the hull just below the hangar deck, aft of the sponson.

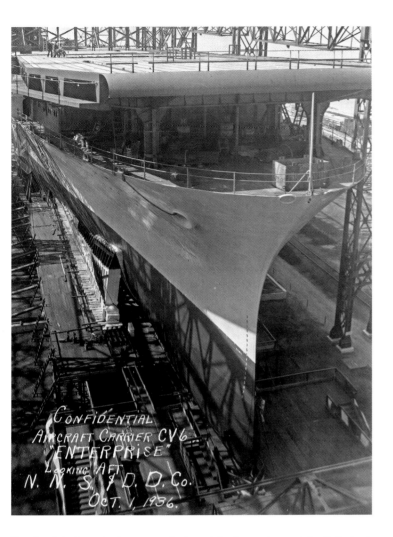

Details of the bow, the forecastle deck, and the forward part of the flight deck are revealed in this October 1, 1936, photograph. Draft marks, for gauging the depth of the hull when fully afloat, are painted on the side of the bow.

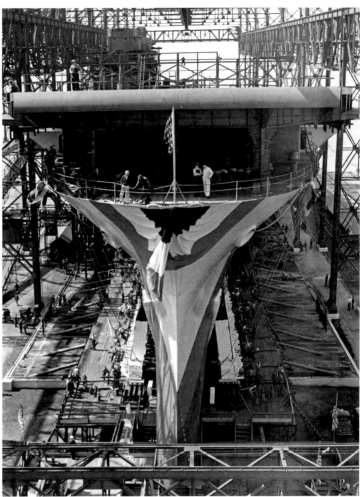

The aircraft carrier *Enterprise* was launched at Newport News Shipbuilding and Dry Dock Company, Newport News, Virginia, on October 3, 1936. Prior to the launching ceremony on that day, the ship is viewed from the front, at the level of the flight deck. The jack is waving from the forecastle, and red, white, and blue bunting has been fastened to the bow.

Mrs. Lulie Lyons Hall Swanson, the wife of Secretary of the Navy Claude A. Swanson, was the sponsor of the *Enterprise*. She is seen here, *third from left*, on launching day.

USS *Enterprise* Data

Ordered	August 5, 1933
Laid down	July 16, 1934
Launched	October 3, 1936
Commissioned	May 12, 1938
Decommissioned	February 17, 1947
Stricken	October 2, 1956
Builder	Newport News Shipbuilding & Dry Dock Co.
Class	*Yorktown*
Sponsor	Mrs. Lulie H. Swanson
Displacement, standard	19,800 tons
Displacement, full load	23,500 tons
Length, waterline, full load	770 feet
Length, hull	809 feet
Length, flight deck	816 feet
Length, overall	824 feet, 9 inches
Beam, waterline, full load	83 feet, 2½ inches
Beam, maximum	109 feet, 6¼ inches
Design draft	24 feet
Bunker fuel	4,280 tons
Endurance (design)	12,500 nautical miles @ 15 knots
Boilers	9 Babcock & Wilcox, 400 psi
Machinery	4 Parsons geared turbines, 120,000 total shaft horsepower
Speed	32.5 knots
Armor	4"–2.5" belt; 60-pound protective deck(s); 4" bulkheads; 4" (side)–2" (top) conning tower; 4" (side) over steering gear
Armament, as built:	8 single 5"/38-caliber gun mounts; 4 quad 1.1"/75-caliber machine gun mounts; 24 .50-caliber machine guns
Armament, October 1942	8 single 5"/38-caliber gun mounts; 1 quad 1.1"/75-caliber machine gun mount at bow; 4 quad 40 mm mounts; 32 20 mm Oerlikon guns; 16 .50-caliber machine guns
Radar (1941)	RCA CXAM-1
Aircraft:	90+
Aviation gasoline	177,950 gallons
Aviation facilities	3 elevators; 2 flight-deck and 1 hangar-deck hydraulic catapults
Crew in 1941	ship, 86 officers and 1,280 enlisted; air wing, 141 officers and 710 enlisted

Mrs. Swanson, next to the microphones, has just swung the ceremonial bottle of champagne, *right*, against the bow, to christen the ship. Upon the christening, the remaining tethers securing the ship were released, allowing the carrier to slide down the ways and into the water.

Following its launching, the *Enterprise* was towed to a dock at the Newport News Shipbuilding and Dry Dock Company for its fitting out: the process in which the ship was completed and ready for service with the Navy. The *Enterprise*'s fitting-out period was longer than that of many capital ships, lasting over nineteen months. Here, the *Enterprise* (*right*), and its sister ship *Yorktown* are being fitted out on January 4, 1937. Note the big hammerhead crane looming above *Enterprise*'s island.

CONFIDENTIAL
Aircraft Carrier CV6
"ENTERPRISE"
PORT BOW
N.N.S. & D.D.Co.
JAN. 4, 1937.

In an aerial view over the Newport News Shipbuilding and Dry Dock facility on February 8, 1937, from left to right are three ships being fitted out: the light cruiser USS *Boise* (CL-47), the *Enterprise*, and the *Yorktown*. The *Yorktown* was launched six months before the *Enterprise* and, consequently, was more advanced in its fitting out.

By April 1, 1937, the *Yorktown* had been moved from the fitting-out dock, allowing an unimpeded view of the *Enterprise* from off its starboard bow. Most of the scaffolding had been removed from around the island, exposing to view the smokestack, the tripod mast, and, at the upper front of the island, the pilothouse.

On the same day the preceding photo was taken, this view was made off the *Enterprise*'s starboard stern. Four 5-inch/38-caliber antiaircraft guns with canvas covers have been mounted on the gallery deck: two forward and two aft. There were four more of these guns on the port side of the gallery deck.

Enterprise (right), and Yorktown are at their fitting-out dock at Newport News on July 1, 1937. The previous month, the Enterprise had spent time in a nearby drydock.

Also taken on July 1, 1937, is this view of Enterprise (left) and Yorktown from astern, with the huge hammerhead crane between them. Some scaffolding is present around the island of the Enterprise, and rigged on the hull are staging planks and access ladders for painters.

Its bow freshly painted, *Enterprise* is moored along the fitting-out dock at Newport News on October 1, 1937: two days shy of the first anniversary of its launching. Seven more months of work lay ahead until the ship was commissioned. Repainting of the hull is underway amidships.

As seen from the aft port quarter on October 1, 1937, repainting is underway on the hull, with dark-toned primer being abundant. Note the staging planks suspended from the hull, forward of the large area of dark primer and just above the waterline. Eyebolts were permanently attached to the hull at intervals for the purpose of rigging planks, for the use of sailors or workmen during the frequent periods of hull repairs and maintenance. Note the temporary shed on the flight deck amidships.

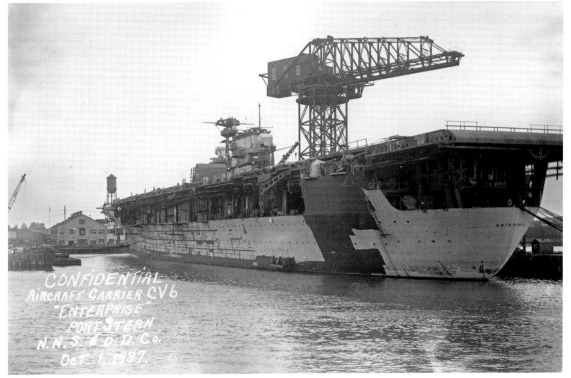

A month and twelve days before its commissioning, *Enterprise* is substantially completed, at Newport News on April 1, 1938. The large shape above the smokestack is the hammerhead crane on the fitting-out dock.

CONFIDENTIAL
AIRCRAFT CARRIER CV6
"ENTERPRISE"
PORT BOW
N.N.S. & D.D.Co.
APRIL 1, 1938.

CONFIDENTIAL
AIRCRAFT CARRIER CV6
"ENTERPRISE"
PORT STERN
N.N.S. & D.D.Co.
APRIL 1, 1938.

Enterprise is viewed from off the port stern on April 1, 1938. The long pole diagonally stored on the hull is a boat boom, to which small boats could be moored when the boom was swung out and secured. Note the motor launch stored on the rear of the forecastle deck, below the flight deck.

The carrier *Enterprise* is lying in the James River in Virginia after a contractor's preliminary trial on April 6, 1938. During preliminary trials, the builder put the ship through its paces to assess its performance and diagnose any problems that required repairs, prior to delivering the ship to the US Navy. Two admiral's barges and two nested motorized launches are stored in the bays toward the rear of the hangar deck.

U.S.S. ENTERPRISE (CV6)
BROADSIDE VIEW
JAMES RIVER, NEWPORT NEWS, VA.
1938, APRIL 6-TH.
LAYING IN STREAM AFTER CONTRACTORS
PRELIMINARY TRIAL.

The *Enterprise* is viewed from off the port bow while lying in the James River after a preliminary trial on April 6, 1938. An unidentified flag, possibly that of the shipbuilder, waves from the foremast, while the US flag is flying from the trunk. On the top of the pilothouse at the upper front of the island are, *front*, a rangefinder, and, *rear*, the forward 5-inch gun director and rangefinder, with a canvas cover over the front of it. A similar director and rangefinder was on the upper rear of the island.

U.S.S. ENTERPRISE (CV6)
PORT BOW VIEW
JAMES RIVER, NEWPORT NEWS, VA.
1938. APRIL 6-TH.
LAYING IN STREAM AFTER CONTRACTORS
PRELIMINARY TRIAL.

CHAPTER 2
Prelude to War

Following its commissioning, USS *Enterprise* underwent a shakedown cruise to South America. It is seen here on August 26, 1938, anchored in Rio de Janeiro harbor, Brazil. Spotted on the forward end of the flight deck with wings folded are Douglas TBD-1 Devastator torpedo bombers. On the aft end of the flight deck are biplanes: either Curtiss BC-3 Helldiver dive-bombers or Grumman F3F-2 fighters.

Nineteen months and tens of thousands of man-hours of labor later, the workers at Newport News completed the fitting out of *Enterprise*, and it was ready for commissioning, the formal induction of the ship into the US Navy fleet. This event took place on May 12, 1938, with Capt. Newton H. White Jr. taking command.

With its commissioning, *Enterprise* became United States Ship (USS) *Enterprise* and was now officially a unit of the US Navy.

Although now a warship, there were still details to be completed on the ship, and the scores of men who would make up its crew labored to become intimately familiar with the ship that was to be their home.

Trials periodically took *Enterprise* into the bay. On one such sojourn on June 15, 1938, Lt. Cmdr. Alan P. Flagg, the ship's air officer, made the first takeoff from *Enterprise*'s decks when he flew Plane No. 1, a Vought O3U-2 (Bureau Number [BuNo] 9312), off the ship, circled around, and two minutes later returned and made history again, recording the first landing aboard *Enterprise*. Later that day, the same aircraft was involved in the first landing accident aboard the ship. At the controls at that time was ACMM J. C. Clarke, who was returning to land at 1130. The landing signal officer's (LSO's) "low" signal did not elicit a response from Clarke, who was then given a wave-off. Clarke applied full throttle and attempted to go around, but due to low altitude, the fuselage and tailwheel struck the ramp. Clarke closed the throttle, and the tailhook snagged a wire, bringing the battered aircraft to a stop.

By June 30, 1938, *Enterprise* had eighty-one aircraft aboard, consisting of twenty Grumman F3F-2s, two O3U-3s, and one Curtiss SBC-3 of Fighting Squadron (VF-6); thirteen Northrop BT-1s of Bombing Squadron (VB-6); twenty Curtiss SBC-3s of Scouting Squadron (VS-6); and twenty Douglas TBD-1s of Torpedo

Squadron (VT-6). In addition, its Utility Unit comprised two more O3U-3s, two Grumman J2F-1s, and a TBD-1.

On July 18, 1938, *Enterprise* left its mooring at Pier 7, Naval Operating Base Norfolk, and began its shakedown cruise, arriving at Ponce, Puerto Rico, on July 23. From there it steamed to Gonaïves Bay, Haiti, arriving July 27, and then on to Guantánamo Bay, Cuba, conducting operations there from July 31 to August 12.

Enterprise crossed the equator for the first time on August 20, pausing briefly for the time-honored Neptune party, before arriving at Rio de Janeiro, Brazil, where it remained from August 25 through September 3.

Sailing for home, it stopped again from September 14 to 17, then made its way northward, passing through storm-ravaged seas off Cape Hatteras before tying up in Norfolk, where post-shakedown repairs were made.

Enterprise fought the seas once again as it finished its trials off New England from October 29 through November 3. During these trials, on October 30 it anchored in Cape Cod Bay south of Provincetown, Massachusetts, before visiting Boston on October 31 and November 1. It returned to Norfolk on November 3.

Capt. White, who became ill, was relieved by Capt. Charles A. Pownall on December 21.

Training exercises began early in the new year, with *Enterprise* and its sister ship *Yorktown* taking part in a series of exercises beginning January 4, including the protection of a convoy in the Caribbean. *Enterprise* dropped its anchor at St. Thomas in the Virgin Islands on January 8 and returned to Gonaïves Bay on January 19, where *Enterprise* and *Yorktown* joined Aircraft, Battle Force, Carrier Division 2, and participated in Fleet Problem XX.

One of the significant lessons learned during this exercise was that aircraft carriers needed larger complements of fighters, so that fighters could both provide air cover for the ships and escort aircraft striking the enemy. Unfortunately, budget constraints and opposing views kept this lesson from being taken to heart until after the US Navy was thrust into battle almost three years later.

Off Hampton Roads, Virginia, on April 12, 1939, *Enterprise* joined *Lexington*, *Ranger*, and *Yorktown* in participating in a fleet review. Originally scheduled to go to New York for the World's Fair, instead *Enterprise* was ordered to the Pacific. Leaving Norfolk on April 20 in company with *Lexington* and *Yorktown*, *Enterprise* anchored in Limon Bay off Colón at the Panama Canal Zone on April 26. It passed through the canal the next day, leaving the Atlantic waters for over six years. After repairs in Balboa, it resumed steaming on May 2 and reached its new home port of San Diego, California, on May 12.

While operating in the waters off California, *Enterprise* made history when, during an exercise in September, Adm. James O. Richardson, Commander Battle Force, US Fleet, deployed it with a pair of destroyers to serve as plane guards at the center of a fleet formation. Four battleships, seven cruisers, and eighteen destroyers steamed in three concentric circular patterns at 1-mile increments to protect the carrier with their antiaircraft guns. "I believe that this was the first time," Richardson recalled, "that both of the following occurred: 1. the carrier occupied the key spot in a cruising formation; 2. all anti-aircraft resources of the formation were disposed for the protection of the carrier."

The following month, *Enterprise* was one of the ships that sailed for Pearl Harbor, arriving on October 12 to begin a monthlong exercise. *Enterprise* remained in Hawaiian waters until February 2, when it steamed for the West Coast. Docking briefly in San Diego, the carrier soon made its way to Puget Sound, arriving on February 21 and entering Navy Yard Puget Sound for overhaul on February 25. The overhaul was completed on May 24, and four days later it steamed for San Diego.

A month later, *Enterprise* steamed toward Hawaii once more, arriving at Lāhainā Roads on July 9, 1940. On July 13, it took aboard an MGM film crew, who filmed portions of the movie *Flight Command* on July 16–17. This would not be *Enterprise*'s only appearance on the silver screen. The ship continued to operate in Hawaiian waters until November 9, during which time it was visited by Secretary of the Navy Frank Knox. The transit from Hawaii to California took five days, and following two weeks in San Diego, *Enterprise* steamed for Puget Sound for degaussing as well as antiaircraft gun installations.

Shipyard work complete, *Enterprise* returned to California and resumed training exercises before leaving for Hawaii on February 19, carrying, in addition to its own air group, thirty Army Air Corps P-36A Hawks bound for Wheeler Field on Oahu.

The carrier returned to Puget Sound on March 3 for a limited overhaul, including degaussing. This work, expedited by order of Adm. Stark, was completed, and *Enterprise* left Puget Sound on March 31, steaming to San Diego.

There it took aboard a Warner Brothers film crew and the stars of *Dive Bomber*, a motion picture that was released in August 1941. Filming aboard *Enterprise* was accomplished in April, and many of the ship's crew can be seen in the film.

After the conclusion of filming, from April through November *Enterprise* made repeated trips between California and Hawaii, taking part in many maneuvers in Hawaiian waters.

In late November, *Enterprise* was tasked with ferrying Marine F4F-3 Wildcats to Wake Island, crossing the international date line en route. The crew had become somewhat accustomed to ferry voyages, but this one was different. At the conclusion of this trip, *Enterprise* was scheduled to put into Bremerton for overhaul, arriving on December 13 and thus providing the crew Christmas stateside. War tensions were rising, and when the ship left Hawaii for Wake on November 28, Capt. George D. Murray, commanding the *Enterprise*, issued Battle Order No. 1, with the approval of VAdm. William F. Halsey. That order read:

1 The ENTERPRISE is now operating under war conditions.
2 At any time, day or night, we must be ready for instant action.
3 Hostile submarines may be encountered.
4 The importance of every officer and man being specially alert and vigilant while on watch at his battle station must be fully realized by all hands.
5 The failure of one man to carry out his assigned task promptly, particularly the lookouts, those manning the batteries, and all those on watch on the deck, might result in great loss of life and even loss of the ship.
6 The Captain is confident all hands will prove equal to any emergency that may develop.
7 It is part of the tradition of our Navy that, when put to the test, all hands keep cool, keep their heads, and FIGHT.
8 Steady nerves and stout hearts are needed now.

Halsey also ordered radio silence, and, fortuitously, that the aircraft be armed from then forward. Murray ordered the ship darkened at night. The Marine fighters left the *Enterprise*'s deck on the morning of December 2, 1941. Shortly after the last of the Marines had lifted off, the ship swung around and headed back to Pearl Harbor, where it was due to return on the afternoon of December 6.

On May 12, 1938, the *Enterprise* was commissioned in a ceremony in which the ship entered active service with the US Navy. At the same time, the designation "USS" (United States Ship) was added to its title. In this photo, apparently taken on *Enterprise*'s commissioning day, the carrier is to the left, while a battleship, very likely USS *New York* (BB-34) is on the opposite side of the dock. Crewmen in dress uniforms are lined up on the dock. *National Museum of Naval Aviation*

Tugboats are assisting the *Enterprise* to its berth at Pier 4 at the US Navy Yard, Norfolk, Virginia, on November 3, 1938. The carrier then underwent a period of postcommissioning repairs and maintenance. No aircraft are present on the flight deck, since normal practice was to fly the air group of an aircraft carrier to land bases while the ship was in port. The original paint scheme of the vertical surfaces above the waterline of the carrier was #5 Standard Navy Gray. The last plane appears to be still on the pier while the crane aft of the island has just deposited the second-from-last plane on to the amidships elevator. *Norfolk Navy Yard*

In a general view of Pier 4 at Norfolk Navy Yard on December 1, 1938, USS *Enterprise* is on the right side of the photo. *Enterprise*'s sister ship *Yorktown*, distinguished by the large letter *Y* on the side of the smokestack, is moored in the background. On the afterpart of the flight deck of the *Enterprise*, the housing mast is raised, with the US flag flying from it. Aft of the island is a crane for handling boats and aircraft. *Norfolk Navy Yard*

USS *Enterprise* is departing from Pier 4 at Norfolk Navy Yard on December 31, 1938. The ship on the opposite side of Pier 4, to the left, very likely was USS *New York* (BB-34), which is known to have been docked alongside the *Enterprise* at Norfolk at one point in 1938. *Norfolk Navy Yard*

U.S.S. ENTERPRISE
DEPARTURE FROM PIER NO. 4
NORFOLK NAVY YARD   PORTSMOUTH, VA.
SERIAL NO. 262 (39)   DEC. 31, 1938

Tugboats have moved the *Enterprise* from Pier 4 out into the Elizabeth River off Norfolk Navy Yard on December 31, 1938. On January 4, 1939, the *Enterprise* and the *Yorktown* would commence joint exercises in the Atlantic and the Caribbean, lasting until April 1939. *Norfolk Navy Yard*

Douglas TBD-1 Devastator, Bureau Number (BuNo) 0323, from Torpedo Squadron 6 ("Torpedo 6," or VT-6), approaches USS *Enterprise*, followed by its plane guard, the destroyer USS *Ralph Talbot* (DD-390), on January 13, 1939.

In April 1939, USS *Enterprise* received orders to join the Pacific Fleet. In September of that year, the US Navy beefed up its forces at Pearl Harbor, on Oahu, in response to increased tensions with Japan. The *Enterprise* was transferred from its home base at San Diego, California, to Pearl Harbor. The carrier is seen here on October 8, 1939, around the midpoint of its voyage from San Diego to Pearl Harbor. Among the many planes spotted on the flight deck are, *to the rear*, Douglas TBD-1 Devastator torpedo planes of Torpedo Squadron 6 (VT-6). Farther forward are Northrop BT-1s, several Grumman J2F Duck floatplanes, Curtiss SBC Helldivers, and Grumman F3F fighters.

The *Enterprise* appears to have been painted recently in this aerial photo of the carrier at sea in January 1940. During this period, the abbreviation "EN" was painted on the forward and the rear areas of the flight deck, so aircraft pilots could easily identify the ship.

USS *Enterprise* is viewed from above during a visit to San Diego in June 1940, following an overhaul at Puget Sound Navy Yard, Washington, that had lasted from February to May 1940. During this period, the flight deck was stained a mahogany brown color, with chrome yellow markings, including the "EN" designations on the front and the rear of the deck. The air group is being craned aboard from the pier. The last plane appears to be still on the pier while the crane aft of the island has just deposited the second-from-last plane on to the amidships elevator.

Secretary of the Navy Frank Knox paid an official visit to USS *Enterprise* at sea in Hawaiian waters in early September 1940 and was in attendance at this religious service conducted on the hangar deck on the eighth of that month. Visible to the upper left are two fighter-plane fuselages, secured to the overhead. This practice was known as tricing, which enabled the storage of more airframes than could be accommodated on the hangar deck.

At the conclusion of his visit to USS *Enterprise* on September 8, 1940, Secretary of the Navy Frank Knox is seated in the rear seat of the Curtiss SBC-4 Helldiver assigned to the air group commander of the *Enterprise*, prepared for the return flight to Oahu.

Religious observances have always been a key part of life aboard a US Navy ship, and *Enterprise* was no exception. Here, with Christmas trees as a backdrop, a choir and orchestra are performing during a midnight mass on Christmas Eve 1940 on the hangar deck. Several civilians are in attendance.

In April 1941, some scenes for the Hollywood motion picture *Dive Bomber*, starring Errol Flynn and directed by Michael Curtiz, were filmed aboard the *Enterprise* at San Diego. In this scene, returning air crews, including some "wounded," are making their way across the flight deck. In the background is Vought-Sikorsky SB2U-2 Vindicator BuNo 1333, with side numbers for Bombing Squadron 3 (VB-3).

Aviation metalsmiths on the hangar deck of the *Enterprise* are assembling a Grumman F4F Wildcat from Fighting Squadron 3 on October 38, 1941. Several aircraft are triced from the overhead.

CHAPTER 3
Off to War

While *Enterprise*'s men planned on a pleasant Saturday night in Hawaii, Mother Nature had other plans, and in retrospect few of the men would complain. Steaming back from Wake, *Enterprise* and its eleven escorts encountered a storm. The storm was of little consequence to the aircraft carrier and the three cruisers with it, but life aboard the eight fuel-starved destroyers accompanying them became miserable. Halsey, a former destroyer man, recognized their plight and ordered the task force slowed.

At 0615 Sunday, air group commander Howard "Brigham" Young, in an SBD of Scouting Six, took off from the deck of the *Enterprise* headed for Ford Island with Lt. Cmdr. Bromfield Nichol, Halsey's assistant operations officer, in the rear seat, entrusted to deliver a classified report concerning Wake Island to Adm. Kimmel. Twelve minutes later, the rest of Scouting Six took off, flying a watchful search pattern that would end with the aircraft landing at Pearl Harbor eight hours earlier than *Enterprise* itself could traverse the 225 miles.

At 0820, when Young was approaching the Marine Corps Air Station at Ewa, he knew something was amiss. Aircraft were circling, and puffs of exploding flak could be seen over the air station and Pearl Harbor. Briefly, he considered that this was an unusual training exercise, but when his aircraft was attacked, the reality of war closed in. Young managed to land; some of the other *Enterprise* fliers were not so lucky. The Japanese had taken a toll on Scouting Six, and that evening a half-dozen Fighting Six F4F-3A Wildcats of the *Enterprise*, which had been searching for the enemy and lacked the range to return to the ship, attempted to land at Ford Island. Four of the Wildcats were shot down by overzealous antiaircraft fire, and three of their pilots were killed.

When *Enterprise* reached Oahu, rather than entering Pearl Harbor it had its escorts steam off the coast in hopes of either finding the enemy or warding off another attack.

Low on fuel and needing to reprovision, *Enterprise*, as the sun sat on December 8, slipped into the battle-scarred harbor.

Fueled by adrenalin and urged by chief petty officers (CPOs), the men of the *Enterprise* refueled and restocked the ship, routinely a twelve-hour job, in less than eight. At 0400 on December 9, it headed back out to sea. The Japanese had hoped to destroy the American carriers at Pearl Harbor. Fortunately, all the carriers had escaped, and now the hunted became the hunter.

The Japanese submarine *I-70* became its first victim. Lt. Clarence Earle Dickinson Jr., who had been shot down over Pearl Harbor and whose gunner, Bill Miller, had been killed on December 7, spotted *I-70* on the surface. Braving antiaircraft fire, Dickinson dropped a 500-pound bomb close amidships the enemy sub, sinking it.

Enterprise's hunting became more aggressive on February 1, when its aircraft struck Japanese installations in the Marshal Islands. Four strikes were launched that day, targeting Kwajalein, Maloelap, and Wotje Atolls. *Enterprise* remained on station for fourteen hours, launching 158 sorties. As the carrier withdrew, a striking force of five Japanese Nell bombers found the *Enterprise*. Although none of their bombs found their mark, one near miss badly injured 2nd Class Bos'ns Mate George Smith, who died two days later, becoming the first *Enterprise* crewman to die at the hands of the enemy. The same blast that critically injured Smith also perforated an external gasoline line, and the ensuing fire consumed paint, canvas, rope, rubber and damaged electrical circuits between frames 130 and 144 before damage control parties could smother it.

One of the *Enterprise* men who fought off the enemy that day was AMM2c Bruno P. Gaido, who, seeing a damaged Nell making a suicide run from astern, leapt into a Dauntless and opened fire with its rear guns. The wing of the Nell bisected the Dauntless,

Although postwar intelligence indicated that the raids were not as successful as they were thought at the time, they were nonetheless successful and provided the US with a much-needed morale-boosting victory.

Aft of the island of the *Enterprise*, an officer supervises as crewmen prepare to transfer fuel lines to USS *Platte* (AO-24), a Cimarron-class fleet oiler that has come alongside to refuel the carrier, in the Pacific on January 1, 1942. Flexible hoses for transferring the fuel are rigged from the *Enterprise*'s boat crane.

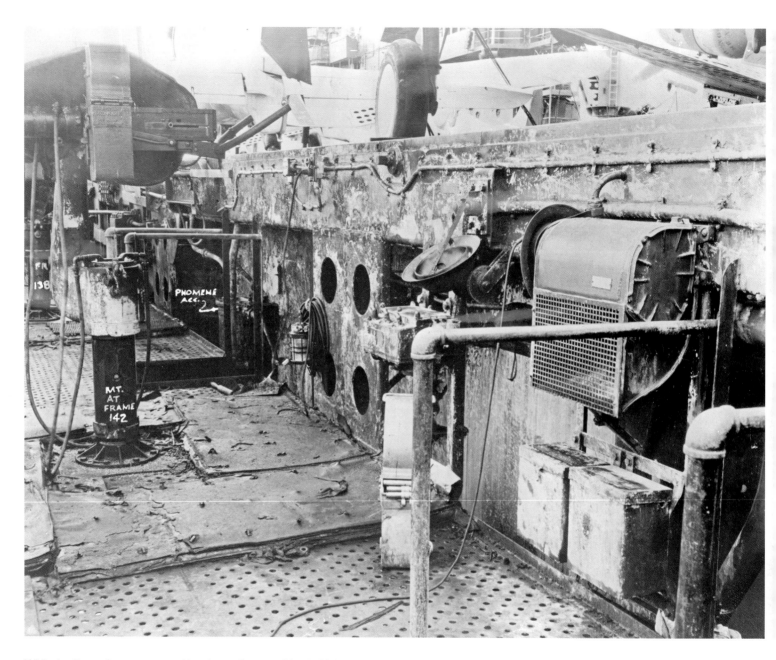

While the *Enterprise* was approaching the northeastern Marshall Islands on a raid against Japanese installations around 1340 on February 1, 1942, five Japanese bombers attacked it. The aircraft didn't register any direct hits on the carrier, but bomb fragments damaged a port bulkhead and a roller curtain of the hangar deck and also ruptured an external fuel line, causing a fire that resulted in damage. A view taken at around frame 144 facing forward shows a .50-caliber antiaircraft machine gun gallery on the port side of the ship that was damaged by the flames.

A Douglas SBD-2 Dauntless dive-bomber on an elevator on USS *Enterprise* is ascending to the flight deck in preparation for the raid on Japanese-occupied Wake Island on February 24, 1942. A dark-colored cover is over the canopy. The national insignia was the early-war type, with a red circle at the center of a white star over a blue circle.

Crewmen are manning one of the quadruple 1.1-inch gun mounts on the *Enterprise* during the Wake Island raid of February 24, 1942. These guns had proved to be ineffective in antiaircraft combat by this time, lacking the volume of fire, range, and explosive punch required to defeat the increasingly fast and nimble aircraft the Japanese were deploying. The 1.1-inch guns also were prone to jamming. More powerful 40 mm antiaircraft guns soon would replace them.

During an attack by Japanese bombers on the *Enterprise* while the carrier was conducting a raid on the Marshall Islands on February 1, 1942, Aviation Machinist's Mate 2nd Class Bruno P. Gaido jumped into the rear cockpit of an SBD of Scouting Squadron 6, parked on the flight deck of the carrier, and fired the flexible machine guns at an incoming Japanese bomber. Skimming the flight deck, the bomber tore off the tail of the SBD, as shown here, before crashing into the Pacific. Gaido survived the incident, only to be captured and killed by the Japanese in the Battle of Midway, four months later.

Crewmen take a break alongside the two quadruple 1.1-inch gun batteries aft of the island of the *Enterprise* around March 1942. These guns had water-cooled barrels and fired high-explosive projectiles with a super-quick fuse. Each gun had a practical rate of fire of about 100 rounds per minute; the projectiles had a maximum range of about 7,400 yards and a maximum ceiling of about 6,300 yards. To the left is the lower part of the main boat crane. At the very bottom of the photo, aft of the walking sailors is the forward edge of the torpedo elevator.

In mid-March 1942, the *Enterprise* was docked at Pearl Harbor for various modifications and repairs, including installation of additional radar units; the repair of decking and boilers 7, 8, and 9; and the removal of ten boats. A key modification was the replacement of the .50-caliber antiaircraft machine guns by the far more potent 20 mm cannons. This March 19, 1942, photo depicts the new platform and splinter shield for two 20 mm guns on the bow, below the flight deck. A total of thirty 20 mm gun mounts were installed at that time. *Naval History and Heritage Command*

Two newly installed mounts and armored shields for 20 mm guns on the fantail of the main deck are observed from the port side. Below the gun cradles are canvas collector bags for spent cartridge casings. *Naval History and Heritage Command*

A gallery of five 20 mm gun mounts along with an armored splinter shield has been added to the catwalk to the port side of the flight deck of the *Enterprise* between frames 311 and 342, in a photo taken on March 19, 1942. *Naval History and Heritage Command*

Another gallery of 20 mm gun mounts on the port side of the flight deck is viewed from aft. This gallery was farther forward than the one in the preceding photo, being located between frames 132 and 147. The armored shields have not yet been installed on the mounts. *Naval History and Heritage Command*

During the March 1942 overhaul, the boat storage area on the flight-deck level to the starboard side of the island, between frames 85 and 105, was converted to a gallery for eight 20 mm antiaircraft guns. This area is viewed from aft on March 19, 1942. *Naval History and Heritage Command*

While the Marshall Islands attacks had provided a badly needed morale boost for the US, that paled compared to the mission the "Big E," as *Enterprise* had come to be known, would take part in during early April 1942.

At noon on April 8, only a few hours after Bataan fell, *Enterprise*, along with cruisers *Northampton* and *Salt Lake City*, four destroyers, and a tanker, stood out from Pearl Harbor Navy Yard. Its crew, uncertain of the destination, allowed their imagination to run wild as to their destination during three days of northbound steaming. About 0600, just north of Midway, *Enterprise* rendezvoused with its younger sister *Hornet*, its decks laden with Army B-25 Mitchell bombers. *Hornet* too was escorted by two cruisers, four destroyers, and a tanker.

Speculation among the crew was that the bombers were being ferried to a base for reinforcements, but Adm. Halsey, aboard *Enterprise*, ended the speculation when, observing radio silence, he ordered signaled by lamp throughout the combined force, "This task force is bound for Tokyo."

This was a daring raid, deep into Japanese waters, risking two of the nation's precious carriers along with their escorts on a mission to launch the Army bombers against the Japanese home islands, with the bombers not to return to the carriers, which they could not land on, but rather to fly on to friendly bases in China. *Enterprise*'s function was to provide combat air patrol for the task force, as well as scouting for enemy pickets.

After five more days of steaming, one of *Enterprise*'s scout bombers sighted a Japanese picket boat, and that boat also saw the carrier-borne bomber. About an hour and a half later, one of the Japanese pickets sighted the task force and radioed their presence toward Japan. Col. Doolittle and his men launched from *Hornet* earlier than planned, making their already challenging mission even more difficult, but allowing the task force, with the thousands of men aboard, to turn toward Pearl Harbor and escape an angry enemy, now aggressively looking for them.

As mentioned, this raid provided a much-needed morale boost to the Allies but, even more significantly, altered the Japanese strategy, holding more forces near Japan for homeland defense, thereby reducing the forces available for expanding the war in the Pacific.

Safely retuning to Pearl Harbor, *Enterprise* sailed five days later for Coral Sea, but that battle was over before the Big E arrived. Instead,

Enterprise with *Hornet*, operating as Task Force 16, sailed north toward the Ocean and Nauru Islands, under orders from Adm. Nimitz to remain out of reach of enemy attack planes but to allow enemy patrol aircraft to sight the carriers, which they did on May 15, 1942. The intent was to delay Japan's Operation RY, a planned invasion of these islands, which were rich in phosphates needed by the Japanese war machine. The invasion force was modest, with four cruisers and six destroyers, along with minelayers and troop transports. The appearance of the US carriers in the area caused the Japanese to withdraw, with the invasion being postponed until August. With the feint by *Enterprise* and *Hornet* successful, on May 16 Nimitz sent the urgent coded message "Expedite return."

Enterprise docked in Pearl on May 26, with crew and base personnel aware that they had only one day to turn the ship. Fuel, food, and ammunition were hauled aboard, and worn and damaged equipment was hauled off to be replaced by new. In addition, Adm. Halsey, who was ill, was relieved by RAdm. Raymond Spruance.

Enterprise, in company with *Hornet*, again sailing as Task Force 16, left Pearl Harbor on May 28, one day after *Yorktown* put into Pearl and entered drydock. The battle-damaged *Yorktown* was estimated to require ninety days of repair, which was later revised to two weeks to repair only, not to provide the needed overhaul. To this, Adm. Nimitz stated flatly, "We must have this ship back in three days." On May 30 *Yorktown* along with Task Force 17, under command of RAdm. Frank Jack Fletcher, left Pearl to rendezvous with Task Force 16 at Midway. Tactical command of the operation rested with Fletcher. This would be the only time that the three Yorktown-class carriers would operate together.

Nimitz, through the efforts of cryptographers, was aware of the pending Japanese assault on Midway Atoll. The entire Japanese battle plan was on Nimitz's desk, and he intended to make good use of this intelligence bonanza.

Nimitz had at his disposal *Enterprise*, *Hornet*, and the hastily repaired *Yorktown*. The remaining large carrier, *Saratoga*, having just completed repairs on the West Coast, was steaming hurriedly toward Pearl Harbor with a cargo of replacement aircraft, but it was doubtful that it would arrive in time to participate in the coming engagement—and in fact it would not. The main Japanese striking force, under the command of Adm. Chūichi Nagumo, included four fleet carriers as well as three cruisers and twelve destroyers. This force was trailed by an occupation force and covering group divided into two task groups, between them including two light carriers, five battleships, and six cruisers.

At 0900 on June 3, a PBY flying from Midway spotted the Japanese occupation force and erroneously reported it as the main enemy force. This force was brought under attack by land-based aircraft. The next day at 0630, Nagumo launched his attack on Midway. Just over an hour later, a PBY spotted two Japanese carriers, and after receiving this report, TF-16 immediately launched a strike against the Japanese carrier force, as did aircraft from Midway. The land-based aircraft reached the Japanese force first, although their attack did not produce direct damage and came at a heavy cost to the Americans.

At last being made aware of US carriers in the area, Nagumo prepared to attack the US carriers. However, Japanese doctrine at the time required large, coordinated attacks. With much of his aircraft en route to Midway, Nagumo lacked the aircraft, especially fighters, to execute the large attack demanded by their doctrine. Instead, he chose to wait for his returning aircraft.

While the torpedo attacks from the three American carriers brought about no explosive results, they did force the Japanese to take evasive action, further handicapping their launch of aircraft. The American dive-bombers were considerably more successful than had been the TBDs, with *Enterprise*'s aircraft scoring hits on *Kaga* and *Akagi*, Nagumo's flagship. Meanwhile, *Yorktown* deposited three 1,000-pound bombs on the deck of the *Sōryū*, setting it afire.

Hiryū, unscathed, launched a strike force of eighteen Vals and six Zekes at 1258, which found *Yorktown* just over an hour later. Despite the best efforts of its combat air patrol, antiaircraft gunners, and helmsman, *Yorktown* took three bombs in quick succession, one of which damaged the uptakes, snuffing out most boilers. Quick action and hard work by its damage control parties put *Yorktown* back in action, only to be again attacked by the Japanese. During this second attack the Japanese were able to launch four torpedoes, two of which found their mark. Initially abandoned, the next day a salvage party boarded the ship and resumed an effort to save it, but *Yorktown*'s fate was sealed when a Japanese submarine fired two more torpedoes into its hull.

With the three Yorktown-class carriers operating together, and due to the effectiveness of *Yorktown*'s damage control, the Japanese became confused and mistakenly believed that their multiple attacks had been on various US carriers. This allowed *Enterprise* and *Hornet* to operate unscathed, and they ultimately became foster homes for *Yorktown*'s displaced aviators.

The loss of *Yorktown*, especially so soon after the loss of *Lexington* at Coral Sea, was painful. However, in a mere six minutes

Enterprise's air crews had destroyed two enemy aircraft carriers, and *Yorktown*'s another in the same time.

The Japanese, however, had lost the heavy cruiser *Mikuma*, and its sister ship *Mogami* was heavily damaged. Slipping beneath the Pacific waves were *Akagi, Kaga, Hiryū,* and *Sōryū*. While the battle had cost the Japanese navy 110 veteran air crews, more significantly it also cost the Japanese navy over 40 percent of the aircraft mechanics and flight deck crews, as well as the four carriers themselves, which they could not replace.

Capt. George Murray was relieved by Capt. Arthur C. Davis on June 30, 1942. On July 15 *Enterprise* left Pearl Harbor bound for the South Pacific, to join Task Force 61 in Operation Watchtower, the support of the amphibious landings in the Solomon Islands.

This operation began on August 7, with aircraft from the *Enterprise* bombing and strafing enemy positions on Tulagi, just north of Guadalcanal. *Enterprise*'s fighters, along with those of the *Wasp* and *Saratoga*, provided combat air patrol over the Marines landing ashore. During the day, *Enterprise* had 465 launches and recoveries—although not all launched aircraft returned. The Japanese inflicted considerable losses on the American fighters, with the US carriers losing nine Wildcats while downing only two Zeros.

The next day was a repeat of the first, with the US fighters prevailing against lumbering Japanese bombers but suffering terribly at the hands of the skilled Zero pilots. By the end of the day, one-fifth of the US fighter contingent had been lost.

Operation Watchtower differed from the previous US carrier operations and strategy. To this point, the carriers had quickly entered an area, conducted operations in the open seas, and quickly retired. During Operation Watchtower, the carriers were much more like a bombarding surface vessel, or even a fixed airfield. Watchtower had been planned as a three-day operation, but as the second day wore on, Adm. Frank Jack Fletcher became increasingly concerned. His combat air patrols were suffering heavy losses; his smaller ships, maneuvering to escape enemy attack, needed refueling; and his precious carriers were within range of Japanese land-based aircraft.

Thus, to the dismay of the Marines going ashore, Fletcher decided to withdraw twenty-four hours early. The Marines of course complained; not only were they behind schedule unloading their transports, but as a result of poor loading, many of the most-needed supplies were still buried deep within the holds of the transports.

On the night of the eighth, 33 miles from Tulagi off Guadalcanal, Japanese cruisers handed the Allies one of their worst surface warfare defeats of the war, sending four Allied cruisers to the ocean floor in an area that has since come to be known as Iron Bottom Sound.

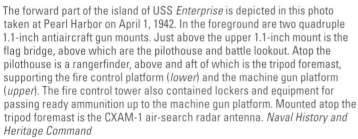

The forward part of the island of USS *Enterprise* is depicted in this photo taken at Pearl Harbor on April 1, 1942. In the foreground are two quadruple 1.1-inch antiaircraft gun mounts. Just above the upper 1.1-inch mount is the flag bridge, above which are the pilothouse and battle lookout. Atop the pilothouse is a rangefinder, above and aft of which is the tripod foremast, supporting the fire control platform (*lower*) and the machine gun platform (*upper*). The fire control tower also contained lockers and equipment for passing ready ammunition up to the machine gun platform. Mounted atop the tripod foremast is the CXAM-1 air-search radar antenna. *Naval History and Heritage Command*

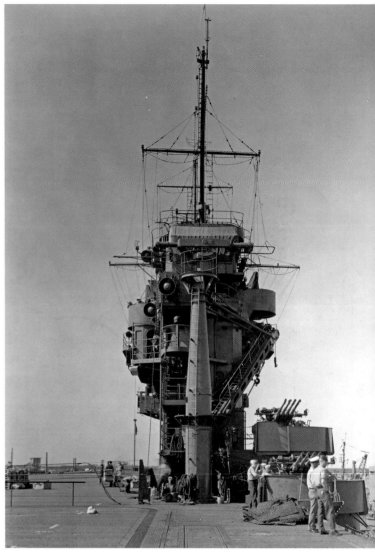

Enterprise's island is viewed from aft at Pearl Harbor on April 1, 1942. Immediately aft of the island is the main boat crane. Visible on the island, above the top of the crane, is the aft Mk. 33 director. The mainmast and foremast and their yardarms and riggings also are in view.

The island of the *Enterprise* is observed from the starboard beam on April 1, 1942. To the far left is the main boat crane, above which on the rear of the island is the aft Mk. 33 5-inch gun director and rangefinder. On the side of the smokestack are two searchlight platforms. The lower platform, near the center of the stack, holds two 36-inch searchlights, while the upper platform has one 24-inch searchlight. Also in view are the tripod mast with the fire control and machine gun platforms, the forward Mk. 33 director, and the pilothouse.

The crews of the two aft port 5-inch/38-caliber antiaircraft guns are on standby as the *Enterprise* conducts a training mission north of the Hawaiian Islands on April 3, 1942. This mission was in preparation for the carrier's role in the forthcoming Doolittle Raid on Tokyo. Douglas SBD Dauntless dive-bombers are secured to the flight deck above the guns.

Following their return from the March 4, 1942, raid on Marcus Island, Douglas SBD Dauntless dive-bombers and, to the front, five Grumman F4F Wildcat fighters are crowded on the forward end of the flight deck of USS *Enterprise*.

An officer and a spotter on the flight deck of the *Enterprise* are observing the fire of 20 mm guns during a training mission in early April 1942. A tracer round from the second gun from the right is visible. The numbers painted on the metal deck side grating indicated the number of feet remaining for launching aircraft.

In a photo dated April 3, 1942, during a training mission north of Hawaii, the crew of a quadruple 1.1-inch gun mount is engaged in a firing drill. The crewmen on the sides of the mount operated handwheels to control the azimuth (traverse) and elevation of the guns.

Following the March 1942 installation of thirty new 20 mm gun mounts on the *Enterprise*, crews are gathered around the 20 mm gun mounts on the starboard side of the island. The drum-shaped magazines that contained ammunition for the guns are not installed.

Plane handlers are pushing a Douglas SBD Dauntless to the side of the flight deck after the engine failed to start on April 17, 1942. The tailwheel is on an outrigger, a device that enabled an aircraft to be stored out of the way, with only its main landing-gear wheels resting on the flight deck.

USS *Enterprise* and escorts departed from Pearl Harbor on April 8, 1942, bound for an April 13 rendezvous in the North Pacific with USS *Hornet* (CV-8), which was carrying sixteen North American B-25 Mitchell medium bombers. These planes, under the command of Lt. Col. James "Jimmy" Doolittle, US Army Air Forces, were destined to deliver the first offensive attack by US forces against the Japanese home islands, on April 18, 1942. Here, in a photo taken from USS *Salt Lake City* (CA-25), the destroyer USS *Fanning* (DD-385) navigates alongside the *Enterprise* on the day of the Doolittle Raid.

Arrestor hook lowered, a Douglas TBD Devastator torpedo bomber is approaching for a landing on USS *Enterprise* on May 3, 1942. Although the Devastator would prove to be a fairly competent bomber, it was too slow and cumbersome to excel in torpedo bombing. Next to the windscreen on the port side of the flight deck, the landing signal officer (LSO) is wielding signal paddles to inform the approaching pilot if he is within the necessary parameters for a successful landing.

LSO Lt. Robin M. Lindsay is using his paddles to signal an approaching pilot as *Enterprise*'s air group returns to the carrier on May 3, 1942. The position of the paddles let the incoming pilot know if he was too high or low, too fast or too slow. If the LSO believed the approaching plane could not make a safe landing, he "waved off" the pilot.

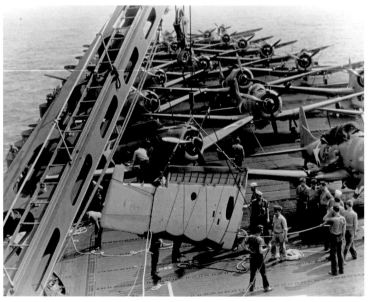

While the fleet oiler USS *Sabine* (AO-25) refuels USS *Enterprise* at sea on May 11, 1942, in the aftermath of the Battle of the Coral Sea, the *Enterprise*'s boat crane is being used to transfer a spare wing to the *Sabine*, for delivery to a land base.

The *Enterprise*'s boat crane, *left*, is hoisting a Grumman Wildcat left wing for transfer to USS *Sabine* on May 11, 1942. Spotted on the flight deck are Douglas SBD Dauntless dive-bombers.

USS *Enterprise* is moored on
Battleship Row at Ford Island,
Pearl Harbor, in May 1942. A fairly
close view is available of the
platform for two 20 mm antiaircraft
guns, on pedestals above the
forecastle. In the left background
is the cage mast of USS *West
Virginia*.

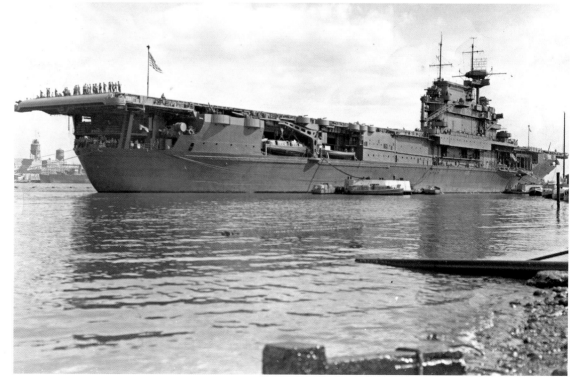

The *Enterprise* is observed off its
starboard stern while moored on
Battleship Row, Pearl Harbor,
during May 1942. Although the
photo is not precisely dated, if the
May 1942 information is correct,
the *Enterprise* was at Pearl Harbor
only from the twenty-sixth to the
twenty-eighth of that month,
following which the carrier sailed
to meet the Japanese fleet at
Midway.

The after part of the flight deck was photographed from a platform on the rear of the island at Pearl Harbor during its brief time there in late May 1942. To the right is a gallery of 20 mm antiaircraft guns with light-colored canvas covers installed, following which is the aft-starboard gallery of two 5-inch/38-caliber antiaircraft guns. The aft 5-inch gun is at full elevation. To the rear of the 5-inch guns is the aft signal platform, with a safety net below it.

This photo of USS *Enterprise* at sea was taken from the cruiser USS *Pensacola* (CA-24) on June 4, 1942, the first day of the Battle of Midway. In the distance is USS *Northampton* (CA-26). The battle that developed that day would pit the air groups of three US aircraft carriers, *Enterprise*, *Hornet*, and *Yorktown*, against four Japanese carriers: *Akagi*, *Hiryū*, *Kaga*, and *Sōryū*.

Douglas TBD Devastators of the ill-fated Torpedo 6 (VT-6) are being prepared for takeoff from *Enterprise* on the morning of June 4, 1942. Although only four of the ship's torpedo planes survived the first day of the battle, *Enterprise*'s dive-bombers sank two of the four Japanese aircraft carriers and participated in the sinking of one other. By the end of the battle, all four Japanese carriers would lie on the bottom of the Pacific.

On the third day of the Battle of Midway, June 6, 1942, Douglas Dauntless dive-bombers from USS *Enterprise*, in coordination with dive-bombers from the *Hornet*, scored crippling hits on the Japanese heavy cruiser *Mikuma*. The stricken cruiser is seen here, dead in the water and on fire, after the aerial attacks. *Naval History and Heritage Command*

A photographer in the rear seat of an SBD from the *Enterprise* took this view of Japanese heavy cruiser *Mikuma* after being bombed by SBDs from the *Enterprise* and the *Hornet* on June 6, 1942. The cruiser took at least five bomb hits from the dive-bombers, knocking out its forward main guns, virtually destroying its bridge, and causing torpedoes to explode, wrecking the amidships area. *Mikuma* ultimately rolled over and sank.

CHAPTER 5
Eastern Solomons, Santa Cruz, Naval Battle of Guadalcanal

After two weeks operating southwest of the Solomons, *Enterprise*, along with *Hornet*, was ordered to intercept a Japanese force that had been spotted 200 miles north of Guadalcanal. The resulting August 24 clash, known as the Battle of the Eastern Solomons, cost the Japanese their light carrier *Ryūjō* and, importantly, turned back a Guadalcanal-bound invasion force. But these victories came at a price, with *Enterprise* taking three direct hits from Japanese bombs, along with four damaging near misses. Seventy-four of its crew were killed, and ninety-five more wounded.

Shipyard workers in Pearl Harbor tended to *Enterprise*'s wounds until mid-October. In addition to repairing the damage caused by the enemy, shipyard workers removed the 1.1-inch quadruple mounts of questionable reliability and replaced them with the larger, more reliable 40 mm Bofors guns. The exception was the bow gun, which although continuing to be a 1.1-inch quadruple mount, was replaced with a mount featuring GE power drive. On the sixteenth, it set sail to again join *Hornet* to form Task Force 61, a goal it would achieve on the twenty-third. RAdm. Thomas C. Kinkaid commanded the task force, and Capt. Osborne Hardison was in command of the *Enterprise*, laden with ninety-five aircraft, as the task force sailed again into the South Pacific.

The Japanese, still bent on retaking Guadalcanal and landing additional troops almost nightly, had an imposing force at sea, centered on four aircraft carriers.

Ten days after *Enterprise* left Pearl Harbor, the two navies would clash just north of the Santa Cruz Islands.

Japanese and American planes passed each other scouring the 200 miles that separated the fleets on the morning of October 26. Two SBDs flown from *Enterprise* by Scouting Ten spotted the Japanese carriers *Shōkaku* and *Zuikaku*, signaled their position, and launched their attack. Other SBDs, hearing the location, flew toward the area to join in and spotted a third Japanese carrier, *Zuihō*, and dove toward the ship, scoring two hits, rendering *Zuihō*'s flight deck useless. About ten minutes after this raid, *Hornet* launched a full strike against the Japanese carriers. Twenty minutes later they were joined by three SBDs, nine TBMs, and eight F4Fs from *Enterprise*. *Hornet*, however, had been spotted, and the Japanese had launched their own strike targeting the Doolittle Raid veteran. The strike groups passed each other, their escorting fighters engaging in a brief melee, with the Zeros targeting Avengers, hoping to blunt the American attack.

The Japanese planes found *Hornet*, attacking with deadly accuracy. *Enterprise*, although nearby, was masked by a rain squall and escaped attention. *Hornet*'s own fliers had found the heavy cruiser *Chikuma* and the carrier *Shōkaku*, Adm. Nagumo's flagship, heavily damaging both.

Enterprise's attack force found a Japanese surface force and attacked a battleship and cruiser but managed only near misses.

At 1030 *Enterprise* emerged from the squall and began recovering its own as well as the disabled *Hornet*'s fliers. Forty-five minutes later, while *Enterprise* prepared to launch another strike, it was found by the Japanese. The Combat Air Patrol (CAP) was ineffective, hampered by poor air control. This left the defense of the ship largely up to *Enterprise*'s own antiaircraft gunners, joined by those aboard escorting battleship *South Dakota*. The gunners were able to bring down half of the attacking Japanese, but the rest bore on.

At 1117 a bomb found home, passing through the forward flight deck and exploding just outside the hull forward, punching 160 holes in the hull, the blast knocking a Dauntless overboard and, with it, Sam Presley AMM 1/c, who was manning the SBD's twin .30-caliber guns.

A few seconds later a second bomb hit, just aft of the forward elevator. Partially detonating in the hangar deck, destroying seven aircraft, the rest of the bomb passed two decks below before exploding, killing forty men, primarily in medical and repair parties.

A couple of minutes later, a third Japanese bomb hit nearby, caving in hull plating and opening two tanks to the sea. At 1120, scarcely three minutes after the first bomb hit, the attack was over.

A second wave of attacking Japanese aircraft targeted *Enterprise* at 1135, this time with torpedo planes. This time the CAP was effective, downing nine of the attackers, while antiaircraft fire bagged three more and forced a fourth to fly into the sea. Only one enemy torpedo was launched, which *Enterprise* avoided.

Additional *Enterprise* and *Hornet* aircraft came aboard during a lull before the third Japanese attack on the *Enterprise* began. At 1220 a flight of eighteen Vals began a glide-bombing attack; one scored a near miss on the *Enterprise*, springing plates and letting seawater in. A second Val scored a hit on the heavily armored no. 1 turret of *South Dakota*, holding station 1,000 yards off *Enterprise*. Though not penetrating the turret, shell splinters killed two men and wounded fifty, including its captain.

Fifteen minutes later the fourth wave of the Japanese attack came in the form of fifteen more Vals. Again, the ship successfully evaded further damage.

With *Hornet* out of action, *Enterprise* was the only nest available for the air groups of both carriers. Its no. 1 elevator was stuck in the up position and its no. 2 was stuck in the down position, leaving only the flight deck available to store airplanes. Skillful LSO Robin Lindsey guided fifty-seven aircraft onto *Enterprise*'s increasingly crowded deck, the final eight catching the no. 1 arresting wire.

Despite a valiant effort of its crew, *Hornet* was lost. Lost too were the destroyer *Porter*, seventy-four US aircraft, and 400 men killed or wounded, but the weakened Japanese fleet was turned back, a cruiser and two carriers were heavily damaged, and, more significantly, 148 flying men were lost, even more severe losses than they had sustained at Midway.

On October 30, *Enterprise*, now the only operational US carrier in the Pacific, reached Nouméa, New Caledonia, tying up next to the repair ship *Vestal*. *Vestal*'s crew, joined by a seventy-five-man Seabee detachment from Company B of the 3rd Construction Battalion and *Enterprise*'s own men, began the arduous task of bringing the carrier back into fighting trim. The repairs were estimated to take three weeks, yet Halsey allowed them only eleven days. Thus, on November 11, *Enterprise* sailed from Nouméa with hull damage still evident, leaking fuel, and

with dozens of Seabees and *Vestal*'s men still aboard, hurriedly trying to complete repairs before the Naval Battle of Guadalcanal erupted two days later.

In the predawn hours of November 13, the battle broke out in a surface action, which pitted two Japanese battleships, a cruiser, and fourteen destroyers under the command of VAdm. Hiroaki Abe against a US force of two heavy cruisers, three light cruisers, and eight destroyers. Although the US ships were technologically superior, with five of them equipped with the latest SG radar, the Japanese had considerably more experience at night fighting, and frankly, the inexperienced US commander, RAdm. Daniel J. Callaghan, was fighting out of his league.

While the US forces suffered tremendous losses, the Japanese had expended much of their bombardment ammunition. This, along with the uncertainty about what other US ships may have been in the area, caused Abe to withdraw his forces without delivering their preinvasion bombardment to Guadalcanal.

When daylight arrived, *Enterprise*'s aircraft, along with Marine Avengers from Henderson Field and Army B-17s from Espiritu Santo, found the Japanese battleship *Hiei*, heavily damaged in the night fighting. The aircraft hammered the ship repeatedly during the day, and *Hiei* sank the following evening.

While *Enterprise* contributed to the sinking of the *Hiei* and remained unscathed, the US fleet did suffer heavy losses, including the light cruiser *Atlanta*, which had been so badly damaged that it had to be scuttled. Also damaged were *Helena* and *Juneau*, the later subsequently torpedoed by a Japanese submarine and sinking in twenty seconds, with a horrific loss of life, including the five Sullivan brothers.

However, the Japanese were not deterred from attempting a massive landing on Guadalcanal; rather, the attack was merely pushed back one day.

A force of cruisers and destroyers from the Japanese 8th Fleet were tasked with bombarding Henderson Field. They were joined by the veteran battleship *Kirishima* and its escorts, as well as the 2nd Fleet. With no US surface vessels in sight, the 8th Fleet approached Guadalcanal uncontested and battered the Marines and others on Henderson Field during the evening of November 13. At dawn, aircraft from the *Enterprise* as well as Henderson Field launched a counterattack, costing the Japanese a heavy cruiser. The remaining action of the engagement, which came to be known as the Naval Battle of Guadalcanal, was surface action, including a gunfight between *South Dakota* and *Washington* versus the Japanese battleship *Kirishima* and its escorts. *South Dakota* was damaged, and *Kirishima* was sunk.

During the Battle of the Eastern Solomons, at around 1712 on August 24, 1942, some thirty Japanese dive-bombers subjected USS *Enterprise* to a concentrated bombardment lasting five minutes. The *Enterprise* suffered three direct hits and four near misses in the attack. A photographer aboard *Enterprise* took this view as the carrier passed by the smoking wreckage of two Japanese bombers shot down during the battle.

The first bomb to strike *Enterprise* on August 24, 1942, penetrated elevator no. 3 at the flight deck, exploding 42 feet below, between the second and third decks. Shown here in a photo taken on September 12, 1942, is the hole where that bomb penetrated the forward starboard corner of that elevator. A 30-inch measuring stick is laid over the opening.

The first bomb hit on the *Enterprise* on August 24, 1942, resulted in a large, upward bulge in the hangar deck at bulkhead no. 173, as seen in this photo from the well of the aft elevator facing forward.

The first Japanese bomb to penetrate *Enterprise* on August 24, estimated to be a 1,000-pound, armor-piercing type with a delayed fuse, exploded to the starboard of the ship's centerline, in the CPOs' quarters, causing extensive damage but not excessive structural damage. Shown here is bomb damage in the galley area of the quarters, facing forward and port.

The second Japanese bomb to hit the *Enterprise* on August 24, 1942, struck thirty seconds after the first one, near the starboard edge of elevator 3 and 11 feet from the starboard edge of the flight deck at frame 179. This bomb had a short-delay fuse and exploded 8 feet below the flight deck, causing that deck to buckle upward 2 feet and also igniting forty powder casings for the 5-inch guns, starting an intense fire. This photo documents the blast of that bomb as it devastated 5-inch/38-caliber gun gallery no. 3.

Crewmen of the *Enterprise* are fighting the fire created by the second bomb to strike the ship during the battle on August 24, 1942. The site is in the 5-inch/38-caliber gun gallery no. 3, to the starboard side of elevator 3. Flight deck damage from the third bomb is also visible.

The detonation of the 5-inch ammunition by the second Japanese bomb to strike *Enterprise* on August 24, 1942, caused the flight deck to bulge upward, inboard of 5-inch/38-caliber gun gallery no. 3, as seen here. Damage to the splinter shield of the gun gallery also is evident. This bomb killed almost forty crewmen instantly.

The space inboard of the 5-inch/38-caliber gun gallery no. 3, where the second Japanese bomb detonated the ammunition, is shown. The view is facing forward. The bomb also crashed through this deck, causing extensive damage to the sheet-metal shop and aviation storeroom below.

This photograph of the explosion of the third Japanese bomb to strike USS *Enterprise* on August 24, 1942, is a still frame from motion-picture footage taken by Photographer's Mate 2nd Class Marion Riley. It struck one minute after the second bomb, on the flight deck at frame 127 near the aft starboard corner of elevator 2. The blast damaged the camera, but Riley survived. Note that the flames from the second bomb hit farther aft.

After the August 24, 1942, attack on the *Enterprise*, crewmen scrutinize the hole in the flight deck from the third bomb. Fortunately, this bomb narrowly missed a torpedo-storage space. The damage to the second and third elevators from the attack left only elevator 1 in operation.

The hole in the flight deck from the third Japanese bomb to strike the *Enterprise* is viewed close-up, with the aft starboard corner of elevator 2 to the right. The second and third bombs to hit the *Enterprise* were estimated to be 500-pound general-purpose types.

Lumber has been emplaced to shore up the starboard bulkhead in the CPOs' quarters on the *Enterprise* following the explosion of the second bomb on August 24, 1942. Mattresses were jammed between the bulkhead and the shoring to limit the amount of water flowing in through the ruptured hull.

USS *Enterprise* is seen from the aft starboard quarter while underway following the attack by Japanese dive-bombers on August 24, 1942. Water is being pumped out of the flooded CPOs' quarters, below the 5-inch/38-caliber gun gallery no. 3. Several Avenger torpedo bombers and Dauntless dive-bombers have been spotted on the flight deck.

In a color photo probably taken during temporary repairs to the *Enterprise* at Tongatapu, Tonga, a few days after the August 24, 1942, attack on the carrier, the wreckage in the aft starboard 5-inch gun gallery is viewed facing forward. In the steel deck is the large hole where the second bomb to strike the ship punched through the deck. On the near side of that hole are smaller entry holes from fragments.

At Tongatapu, Tonga, during temporary repairs to the *Enterprise* a few days after the August 24, 1942, attack, the damage to the flight deck from the second bomb is depicted. The flight deck buckled upward from the slightly delayed blast after the bomb penetrated the flight deck. Toward the left of the damaged area is where the bomb penetrated the deck.

Crewmen of the *Enterprise* are surveying the buckled flight deck between elevator no. 3 and the 5-inch/38-caliber gun gallery no. 3, following the August 24, 1942, dive-bombing attack. Shrapnel from the bomb caused damage to the boat crane in the background, as well as to many other structures.

The part of the starboard side of the hull perforated by bomb fragments from the explosion in the CPOs' quarters, slightly below the waterline, is shown close-up. Inside this damaged area, crewmen rigged wooden shoring and mattresses to stop the mass infiltration of seawater.

The same section of buckled deck shown in the preceding photograph is viewed from the front, facing aft. The tie-down strips, steel strips with C-shaped cutouts for securing aircraft to the deck, are all that remains of part of the elevator.

During the August 24, 1942, Japanese dive-bombing attack on the *Enterprise*, the explosion of a bomb that narrowly missed the aft port quarter of the carrier caused this damage to the degaussing cables along the port stern. Degaussing cables carry electrical current through them to decrease the ship's magnetic field, in order to defeat magnetic mines.

The near-miss bomb explosion off the port stern severed many of the clips holding the four tiers of degaussing cables to the hull, as seen in a photo of *Enterprise* taken in drydock at Pearl Harbor on September 11, 1942. The blast also caused pronounced buckling to the steel plates of the shell of the hull, which nearly ruptured along the line of the third deck.

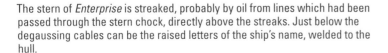

The stern of *Enterprise* is streaked, probably by oil from lines which had been passed through the stern chock, directly above the streaks. Just below the degaussing cables can be the raised letters of the ship's name, welded to the hull.

Following the August 24, 1942, bombing of the *Enterprise*, while still at sea, crewmen made a temporary repair to the shell of the starboard side of the hull along and above the waterline, below 5-inch/38-caliber gun gallery no. 3. That repair is shown on September 11, 1942, after the ship went into drydock at Pearl Harbor.

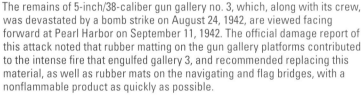

The remains of 5-inch/38-caliber gun gallery no. 3, which, along with its crew, was devastated by a bomb strike on August 24, 1942, are viewed facing forward at Pearl Harbor on September 11, 1942. The official damage report of this attack noted that rubber matting on the gun gallery platforms contributed to the intense fire that engulfed gallery 3, and recommended replacing this material, as well as rubber mats on the navigating and flag bridges, with a nonflammable product as quickly as possible.

Enterprise's 5-inch/38-caliber gun gallery no. 3 is viewed from forward on September 11, 1942. The paint on the guns burned completely off, and the instruments of the guns were destroyed. To the upper right are several exit holes from fragments of the bomb that exploded below that part of the flight deck.

Loose steel plates cover the hole on the flight deck near the aft starboard corner of elevator no. 2, in a September 11, 1942, photograph facing forward. Note the gouges in the wooden planks of the deck, caused by the exploding bomb.

A September 12, 1942, photo depicts details of punctures in the flight deck adjacent to 5-inch/38-caliber gun gallery no. 3. These are exit holes from fragments from the bomb after it exploded belowdecks.

On September 12, 1942, a section of the main, or hangar, deck has been cut away for repairs to the damage caused by the first Japanese bomb to strike the *Enterprise* during the August 24 battle. The view is toward the starboard, with several stanchions along frame 169 appearing to the left. The man at the center is standing on the second deck. Note the bulging of the main deck and the buckled plates on the second deck.

Damage inside the aft starboard gun platform, inboard of 5-inch/38-caliber gun gallery no. 3, is seen facing aft. Slightly above the center of the photo is the entry hole in the flight deck where the second Japanese bomb struck the *Enterprise* on August 24; the hole is faintly visible because a steel plate has been placed over it. Smaller holes from bomb fragments are visible in the flight deck. The ammunition-packing tubes in the background were not present during the August 24 attack.

U.S.S. ENTERPRISE   11 SEPT. 1942   3705-
AFTER STBD. GUN PLAT. LOOKING AFT.   BO
ENTRY HOLE IS VISIBLE IN THE FLIGHT DECK OV
NEAR CENTER OF PHOTOGRAPH.   STOWAGE WAS   N
THERE AT TIME OF EXPLOSION.

This view of the devastation to the aft starboard gun platform was taken from slightly aft of the preceding photo, and facing inboard rather than aft. The second bomb to hit *Enterprise* on August 24, 1942, exploded in this space, 8 feet below the flight deck, causing considerable structural damage and loss of life. The blast buckled the flight deck upward and blew holes through the bulkhead (*right*), and the floor of the gun platform. Secondary explosions of stored ammunition in this area added to the destruction.

During repairs at Pearl Harbor in September 1942, on the hangar deck facing aft and starboard, note the closest two crewmen standing together toward the left. To the right of the right-hand crewman's head, on the lateral bulkhead, no. 173 (in the background), is a jagged hole that the first bomb to hit the *Enterprise* created during its path into the ship. After exiting the bulkhead, the bomb punched its way through the hangar deck before exploding below.

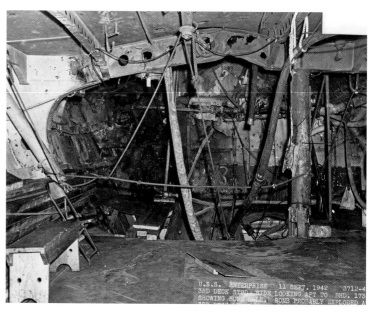

A welder is cutting away damaged areas of the flight deck around the aft-starboard quarter of elevator no. 2 on September 12, 1942. The third bomb to hit *Enterprise* on August 24, 1942, detonated on impact with the flight deck at a point to the left of the welder's head. Elevator no. 2 is to the upper left of the photo, with damage visible on its corner.

Taken on the third deck, facing aft toward bulkhead 173 (in the background), this photo depicts the site where the first bomb to strike *Enterprise* exploded. Note the buckled frame and second deck toward the top of the photo.

During repairs to the bomb damage on USS *Enterprise* at Pearl Harbor on September 12, 1942, a paint fire broke out on the starboard side of the ship, forward of the island. Despite the serious appearance of the fire in this photo, it was not included in the September 1942 damage report of the *Enterprise* and presumably was extinguished before serious damage was done. Repairs on the carrier at Pearl Harbor were completed by October 7, 1942. During this period in the harbor, four of the 1.1-inch gun mounts were replaced by quadruple 40 mm gun mounts, a dozen additional 20 mm gun mounts were installed, and an addition search radar was mounted.

USS *Enterprise* sailed from Pearl Harbor on October 16, bound once again for the Solomon Islands. Ten days later, during the Battle of Santa Cruz, *Enterprise* was once again the target of Japanese bombers, receiving two direct hits from bombs and two near misses. In this photograph taken from off *Enterprise*'s port bow from the cruiser USS *Portland* (CA-33), *Enterprise* is heeling to starboard during an evasive turn during the Japanese attack on October 26, 1942.

Flak bursts are peppering the sky above and beyond the *Enterprise* off the Santa Cruz Islands on October 26, 1942, as it maneuvers to evade bombs and torpedoes dropped by Japanese aircraft. Here again, the photograph was taken aboard USS *Portland*. The view is off the carrier's port beam.

USS *Portland* was off *Enterprise*'s starboard stern when a photographer on the cruiser took this photo of the carrier heeling to starboard during the Japanese attack at Santa Cruz, on October 26, 1942. At least four aircraft are visible on the flight deck forward of the island, and another aircraft has gone over the side of the flight deck near its aft end.

Smoke is boiling up from the flight deck of USS *Enterprise* as a destroyer passes by in the middle distance. The *Enterprise* took two direct hits and two near misses from bombs in the Battle of Santa Cruz.

Water geysers high above the port beam of the *Enterprise* following a near miss of a 250-kilogram bomb on the port side opposite frame 129½ during the battle of Santa Cruz, October 26, 1942.

USS *Enterprise* is viewed from the starboard side during the Japanese attack at Santa Cruz on October 26, 1942. Smoke from a hit or near miss is to the front of the carrier's island. Above and to the front of the bow, just above the clouds, a Japanese bomber is faintly visible.

A Japanese bomber has registered a near miss off the stern of the *Enterprise* on October 26, 1942. At least eight airplanes are visible on her flight deck. *National Archives*

USS *Enterprise* navigates a gauntlet of Japanese bombs on October 26, 1942, as documented by a photographer on the battleship USS *South Dakota* (BB-57). Explosions of antiaircraft shells from the *South Dakota* and other escort ships virtually cover the sky over the embattled carrier. A Japanese aircraft is faintly visible, flying low, midway between the *Enterprise* and the ship to the far left. *National Archives*

The first bomb to strike the *Enterprise* on October 26, 1942, punched through the flight deck at frame 4, 9 feet to the port of the centerline, then punctured the forecastle deck and exited through the port shell above the hangar deck before exploding well above the waterline. In a photo of the ship at anchor after the battle, many holes from bomb fragments are on the port bow; there also are fragment holes on the starboard bow, and those are circled.

The first bomb to penetrate *Enterprise* in the Battle of Santa Cruz, on October 26, 1942, exited through the forecastle, severing in the process the front ends of several of the degaussing cables. Several bomb fragments also punctured the splinter shield for the 20 mm guns above the forecastle. During this attack, the *Enterprise* also took a direct, penetrating bomb hit on its flight deck at frame 44½, causing extensive damage belowdecks. Two near misses also caused damage to the hull below the waterline. Prior to the Battle of Santa Cruz, the forward gun tub had been converted to hold a 1.1-inch gun mount, which is why it has the extra bulge and director as compared to the photo on page 38.

This aerial photograph of the *Enterprise* reportedly was taken on November 10, 1942. If that is accurate, the site was Nouméa, New Caledonia, where the carrier was repaired after the Battle of Santa Cruz.

USS *Enterprise* participated in the Naval Battle of Guadalcanal from November 12 to 15, 1942. This photo of the carrier from starboard reportedly was taken on November 21, 1942. If that date is correct, the location would have been the anchorage at Great Roads, Nouméa, New Caledonia. By this time, the two Mk. 33 directors were fitted with Mk. 4 fire-control radar antennas; these were mounted atop the director housings. Also note the platform jutting from the starboard side of the smokestack, between the forward and center flues; this held a small radar antenna. *US Navy*

This photo of the *Enterprise* also reportedly was taken on November 21, 1942. A floatplane, apparently a Grumman J2F Duck, is on the water aft of the stern of the carrier. During the period from spring 1942 to autumn 1943, the *Enterprise* was painted in a variation of Measure 11 camouflage with 5-N Navy Blue replacing Sea Blue (5-S) on vertical surfaces while retaining Deck Blue (20-B) on horizontal surfaces. This modified scheme began to be used by both the Atlantic and Pacific fleets before the end of 1941, and by June 1942 this derivative was designated Measure 21. At some point since April 1942, one of the two searchlights on the platform at the center of the starboard side of the smokestack had been removed, leaving one searchlight at that location.

In the mail room of USS *Enterprise*, clerks are sorting mail taken aboard at Nouméa, New Caledonia, on December 1, 1942. This shipment of mail, comprising eighty-four bags, contained many Christmas packages and greetings, certain to help bolster crew morale.

Chaplain Merle Young, *foreground*, is conducting a Protestant religious service for officers and crewmen on the hangar deck of the *Enterprise* on Christmas Day, December 25, 1942. The crew had much to be thankful for, with the ship and most of its company having survived several hard-fought battles and achieved important victories during that year. Inside the sloping bulkhead in the distance are the three uptakes as well as three air intakes. Behind the center of the crowd can be seen the pistons and tracks of the midships elevator.

A new, high-performance fighter, the F4U-1 Corsair, began entering service with the US Navy and the Marine Corps in mid-1942, and the aircraft was declared combat ready in late 1942. Here, an F4U-1 with the early, "birdcage," canopy, piloted by Lt. Stanley W. "Swede" Vejtasa, a fighter ace serving with VF-10, has just landed on the *Enterprise* during a series of initial tests of the plane's ability to land and take off from the carrier, in the South Pacific on March 19, 1943. Lt. Vejtasa made two landing approaches before touching down on the flight deck.

Vejtasa's F4U-1 is spotted on the hangar deck following his first day of takeoff and landing trials on the *Enterprise*. With wings folded, the F4U-1 took slightly more space than the then-current fleet fighter, the F4F-4 Wildcat, with its wings folded. Contrary to what has been written post war, the Corsair was found to be suitable for carrier operations, but was instead initially sent to shore-based units for supply chain efficiency Note the aircraft wing in the net above the Corsair.

In April 1943, USS *Enterprise* was based at Espiritu Santo, New Hebrides. The ship is seen here cruising at low speed in a channel off Espiritu Santo on the thirteenth of that month. A few aircraft, including TBF/TBM Avengers, are spotted on the aft part of the flight deck.

For a period in late 1942 and early 1943, a small SC secondary air-search radar antenna was installed on a four-legged pedestal on the forward port corner of the top of the smokestack, as documented in a Berth CV-1, Segond Channel, Espiritu Santo on April 19, 1943.

Machinists are at work in one of the *Enterprise*'s state-of-the-art machine shops in a photograph dated May 3, 1943. According to the original inscription with this photo, the tools and machinery in this shop were worth $50,000: almost $750,000 in current-day dollars. The crewmen in this view include, *far left*, Chief Machinist's Mate E. A. Korn.

In mid-May 1943, USS *Enterprise* arrived at Pearl Harbor in order to undergo permanent repairs to damage below the waterline incurred during the Battle of Santa Cruz. The carrier was in drydock at Pearl from May 18 to 29. Here, on the carrier's first day in drydock, workers on the floor and on staging planks are scraping the starboard side of the hull between frames 23 and 35, where the shell and frames were severely buckled by the near miss of a Japanese bomb during the third attack on the carrier on October 26, 1942. That bomb had detonated 17 feet below the waterline of the carrier, 8 feet out from the outer shell of the hull, opposite frame 30½.

In the Battle of Santa Cruz, another Japanese bomb missed the *Enterprise*, exploding 8 feet below the waterline and 10 feet from the starboard side of the hull opposite frame 129½. This detonation dented the shell plating underneath the belt armor, resulting in flooding to three fuel tanks and shock damage to the no. 2 high-pressure turbine casing. In this photo taken on May 18, 1943, sailors are preparing the crumpled hull around the damaged area for repair. At the bottom is the aft bilge keel. Note the water spouting out of gaps in the hull.

In drydock at Pearl Harbor on May 18, 1943, the *Enterprise* is resting on carefully placed keel blocks, ready for repairs to the hull. The damage to the hull on the starboard side between frames 23 and 35 is visible above the white-clad workers on the drydock floor.

Within a moment of the taking of the preceding photo, the damaged area between frames 23 and 35 on the starboard side of the hull of the *Enterprise* is viewed from aft. These photos provide a good idea of the extent to which the shell and frame of the hull were bashed in by the near miss of a Japanese bomb.

Three days after the preceding photos were taken, on May 21, 1943, shell plates have been removed from the damaged area of the hull of the *Enterprise* between frames 23 and 35, rendering the interior of the hull visible inboard of the scaffolding.

Looking forward and inboard, shell plates and sections of the frame have been removed from the area of the starboard hull damaged by the aft near miss, between frames 123 and 135. Inside the cutout area is a longitudinal bulkhead; at the front of the opening is lateral bulkhead 123.

This May 21, 1943, view shows the same area of damaged hull as the preceding photo, from the opposite end of the cavity.

At Pearl Harbor on May 27, 1943, Adm. Chester W. Nimitz, behind the podium, presents the Presidential Unit Citation to USS *Enterprise*. Receiving the citation is Capt. Samuel P. Grinder, *left*, commanding officer of the ship. This was the first Presidential Unit Citation ever presented to an aircraft carrier, and it praised the crew of the carrier for "consistently outstanding performance and distinguished achievement during repeated action against enemy Japanese forces in the Pacific war area, December 7, 1941, to November 15, 1942."

Nimitz's presentation of the Presidential Unit Citation to the *Enterprise* is viewed from above the flight deck of the ship, on May 27, 1943. Four still and movie cameramen are documenting the ceremony, to the front of the first rank of officers.

Following the May 1943 repairs to the lower hull of the *Enterprise*, the carrier remained based at Pearl Harbor through June and part of July, for further modifications and modernizations. In this photo, taken on June 7, 1943, *Enterprise* is operating in Hawaiian waters. Just below the aft end of the flight deck, on each side of the ramp is a gallery of two 20 mm antiaircraft guns. *US Navy*

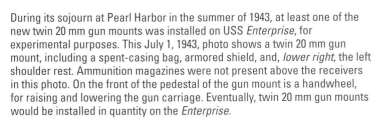

During its sojourn at Pearl Harbor in the summer of 1943, at least one of the new twin 20 mm gun mounts was installed on USS *Enterprise*, for experimental purposes. This July 1, 1943, photo shows a twin 20 mm gun mount, including a spent-casing bag, armored shield, and, *lower right*, the left shoulder rest. Ammunition magazines were not present above the receivers in this photo. On the front of the pedestal of the gun mount is a handwheel, for raising and lowering the gun carriage. Eventually, twin 20 mm gun mounts would be installed in quantity on the *Enterprise*.

Also installed on the *Enterprise* while at Pearl Harbor in the summer of 1943 was this experimental triple 20 mm gun mount. In this July 1, 1943, photograph, Chief Boatswain's Mate Preston is firing the piece, while Gunnery Officer Lt. Cdr. Elias B. Mott II, *left*, observes. Despite the marked increase in firepower the triple 20 mm gun mount offered, compared with that of the single 20 mm piece, the experimental mount did not enter series production.

CHAPTER 6

January 1943–June 1944

Following the Naval Battle of Guadalcanal, *Enterprise* first steamed to Nouméa for further repairs, then spent December and most of January training. On January 28 1943, it sailed for the Solomons again, where its aircraft provided CAP during the Battle of Rennell Island. The carrier then moved to Espiritu Santo, from which it operated for the next three months providing air cover as needed in the Solomons.

On May 1, it steamed for Pearl Harbor, arriving May 8, to spend the next several weeks training airmen. On the twenty-seventh of the month, Fleet Adm. Chester Nimitz boarded the *Enterprise* and presented Capt. Samuel P. Ginder, *Enterprise*'s commanding officer, with the Presidential Unit Citation, in recognition of outstanding performance by the ship, and its aircraft against the armed enemy of the United States.

At long last sailing for the United States for much-needed rest for the men and overhaul of the ship, *Enterprise* tied up at Bremerton, Washington, on July 20, its first stateside docking since September 1939. The crew was divided into thirds, with each third getting thirty days leave in succession.

Beyond that rest, arguably the biggest improvement to come out of its time in the shipyard was the addition of a torpedo blister along three-quarters of its hull. This was intended to prevent it from meeting the fate of its sisters. Additional antiaircraft guns were also fitted, as were improved radar, along with an expanded flight deck. Moving ahead, it would not carry the venerable F4F Wildcat, but instead the powerful F6F Hellcat, the winningest Navy fighter ever.

Leaving Puget Sound on Halloween, by November 6 the carrier was back in Pearl Harbor, and the next day it got a new commander when Capt. Matthias Gardner relieved Capt. Ginder. At the same time, *Enterprise*'s Air Group 6 got a new leader, Edward "Butch" O'Hare. O'Hare, along with Bill Martin, leading Torpedo 10 aboard, began to develop night attack techniques for the *Enterprise*'s aircraft.

Beginning on November 19, *Enterprise* aircraft began striking Japanese positions on Makin Atoll in the Gilbert Islands.

On the twenty-sixth, O'Hare's concept of nighttime hunter-killers was put to the test, a radar-equipped Avenger serving as a guide to a pair of otherwise-blind Hellcats. Unfortunately, during that mission the legendary Medal of Honor recipient O'Hare vanished.

Back at Pearl Harbor in January 1944, *Enterprise* again took aboard Air Group 10, which had spent weeks training for nighttime operations. On the twenty-second of the month, Task Force 58, including *Enterprise*, sailed toward the Marshall Islands. *Enterprise*'s first target was Taroa in Maloelap Atoll. In the predawn hours, eighteen Hellcats were launched from *Enterprise*'s rain-swept decks, two never to be seen or heard from again. Struggling to see the island, much less their targets in the predawn hours, at last contact with the enemy was made when two of the Hellcat pilots spotted four Zeros beneath them and dove for the attack, downing all four. Additional Zeros were spotted by other *Enterprise* pilots, who bagged them just as effectively. As the sun began to rise, the Hellcats saw their intended targets and began to strafe antiaircraft positions at will, paving the way for the bombers that followed. The Big E's aircraft were joined by those from *Belleau Wood* and the new *Yorktown* (CV-10), which continued to pound the Japanese airfield throughout the day.

At dusk, *Enterprise*'s radar detected an expected inbound flight of aircraft. The antiaircraft batteries of the escorting ships opened fire as the bogies drew near, large twin-engine bombers. The CAP dove in, identifying the aircraft as Japanese Nells. Soon, one of the bombers poured flames and crashed into the sea. Jubilation was short-lived when the order to "Cease fire" was sounded. Closer examination had shown that this was a flight of low-flying Army B-25 Mitchell bombers flying from Tarawa. Other than one man, the downed bomber's crew was pulled from the Pacific.

The mighty task force then sailed northward to support the invasions of Kwajalein and Roi-Namur, both of which fell in less than a week. *Enterprise* lost three pilots and four Hellcats, but the ship itself was unscathed.

Enterprise then steamed 1,000 miles to the next target, the Japanese anchorage at Truk, the Imperial Navy's most important base outside the Home Islands. The Americans began their attack in the wee hours of February 16, launching aircraft from *Enterprise* and four of its contemporaries. Only four of the American fighters failed to return to their ships, but the way had been paved for bombers.

That night, men from the *Enterprise* made naval aviation history by conducting the first carrier-based night-bombing attack. Twelve Avengers of Torpedo 10, which despite its name were each armed with four 500-pound bombs rather than unreliable torpedoes, struck Japanese ships in Truk Lagoon. The twelve bombers made twenty-five passes, each typically dropping two bombs per pass. Eleven of the Avengers returned to the *Enterprise*, with Lt. Nicholas's aircraft disappearing, believed downed by antiaircraft fire. Reconnaissance the next day confirmed the reported thirteen hits and seven near misses, revealing eight ships sunk or destroyed and five damaged.

Retiring to Espiritu Santo, *Enterprise* and its men enjoyed a four-day respite before being again ordered into harm's way. The carrier supported Marines landing at Emirau, then sailed 2,700 miles to unleash its aircraft on the Palau islands. In this operation, Avengers and Dauntlesses from the *Enterprise* severely damaged *Wakatake*, a second-class destroyer escorting a convoy on March 30. Later that day, *Yorktown*'s aviators finished the destroyer off.

At the end of April, *Enterprise* supported MacArthur's landings on Hollandia, marking the first time two carriers had supported an Army operation. On April 24 Chick Harmer used one of *Enterprise*'s radar-equipped Corsairs to down a Japanese bomber, damage a second, and drive off the third.

Five days later *Enterprise* again attacked Japanese facilities at Truk, losing a Hellcat and two Avengers in the process. The crews of both were picked up by a Kingfisher operating from USS *North Carolina*, which then taxied the men miles to sea for pickup by a submarine.

After a relatively light May, on June 6, as Allied troops poured ashore halfway around the world at Normandy, *Enterprise* left Majuro bound for the Marianas. It was part of Task Force 58, boasting a whopping 535 ships, including fifteen carriers. On June 12, *Enterprise*'s aircraft struck Saipan and also sank a 1,900-ton Japanese cargo ship.

The attack on Saipan began on June 15, and by June 19 the American and Japanese fleets were near enough to each other that the Japanese launched a sixty-nine-plane strike against the *Enterprise* and its companions.

The carrier was unscathed, but its pilots were very successful. In fact, all of Task Force 58 was successful in what has come to be known as the Marianas Turkey Shoot. TF 58 fighter pilots claimed 400 enemy aircraft, although Japanese records report a more modest but still substantial 260 lost. More significantly, the Japanese carriers *Shōkaku* and *Taihō*, the latter only three months old, had been sunk, both by US submarines. US losses for the day were twenty airplanes.

On the next day, Torpedo 10, on a scouting mission, found another Japanese carrier, relaying its position to the Big E, which along with two other carriers launched a late-day 226-plane, 300-mile strike. Arriving over the Japanese force, which included four aircraft carriers, the Allied aircraft bore in on the attack. When the dust had settled, however, airmen from *Belleau Wood* had sunk the *Hiryo*, *Jun'yō* had been hit twice, and near misses had shaken *Ryūhō*.

In the pitch-black darkness of the vast Pacific night, the American airplanes struggled to find their carrier—or any carrier. Hearing the plaintive calls of his lost airmen, Adm. Marc Mitscher burned himself into the history books, and into the hearts of the airmen and their families, when he issued the simple command "Turn on the lights." Rather than the total blackout conditions normally operated in at night, the powerful searchlights of the fleet snapped on, their powerful beams punching holes straight up through the darkness, visible for 60 miles. Reorienting themselves, the desperate aircraft began to land. When Mitscher saw a *Hornet* plane land on his flagship *Lexington*, he issued his second profound order: "All planes from Commander Task Force 58. Land on any base you see."

As a result, *Enterprise* played host to aircraft from five other carriers, and fifteen of its own planes had found refuge on other decks.

USS *Enterprise* arrived at the Puget Sound Navy Yard, Bremerton, Washington, on July 23, 1943, for a three-month overhaul and modernization. During this stay, the crew was allowed thirty days of leave; this was done in three shifts. Seen here is part of the first of the three sections of the crew to disembark on liberty.

During the *Enterprise*'s yard period at Bremerton from July 23 to September 26, blisters were installed on the hull, between frames 36 and 150, to enhance stability, increase underwater protection, and compensate for previous alterations that had increased the weight of the ship above the waterline. This photo of the forward port section of the hull (along with the following four photos) was taken at Bremerton on October 19, 1943, near the end of the *Enterprise*'s overhaul. The occasion was an inclining experiment, in which the light ship weight, center of gravity, and stability of the ship are established. *National Museum of Naval Aviation*

As seen in a photo of the starboard side from the rear of the island aft, a Mk. 37 director with Mk. 12 fire control antenna has replaced the original Mk. 33 director on the upper rear of the island. Similarly, the forward Mk. 33 director had been replaced by a Mk. 37 director with Mk. 12 antenna. Large weights with numbers painted on them are arrayed on the flight deck for the inclining experiment. *National Museum of Naval Aviation*

Considerable modifications had been made to the forward part of the superstructure at Bremerton in the summer and early fall of 1943. As seen from the starboard side, a new Mk. 37 director with Mk. 12 radar antenna is on the level above the pilothouse. The navigating bridge and pilothouse had been remodeled, and the flag bridge had been removed. *National Museum of Naval Aviation*

The starboard side of the island is seen in closer detail at Bremerton on October 19, 1943. The *Enterprise*'s radar equipment included an SK long-range air-search antenna, an SC-2 secondary air-search antenna, an SM height-finder antenna, and surface-search radar. *National Museum of Naval Aviation*

The port side of the island is depicted on October 19, 1943, at the termination of the modernizations at Bremerton. Just aft of the pilothouse, and jutting from the island, is primary fly control (Pri Fly), an enclosed booth with square windows. On that same level, alongside the rear of the island, is another booth with square windows: this was secondary fly control. When the ship was commissioned, secondary fly was an open bridge at this location; secondary fly was enclosed by April 1940. *National Museum of Naval Aviation*

Its overhaul substantially completed, *Enterprise* navigates in Puget Sound on October 21, 1943. Ten days later, the carrier would be ready to return to sea. During its time at Bremerton, the *Enterprise* had been repainted in Measure 21 camouflage, consisting of Navy Blue (5-N) paint on all surfaces except for decks and horizontal surfaces, which were painted or stained Deck Blue (20-B).

Enterprise is viewed off its starboard beam on October 21, 1943. During its refitting, eight additional 40 mm gun mounts had been installed. Improvements were made to its ventilation and firefighting systems, and the two forward catapults on the flight deck were replaced by improved ones.

On the same date as the preceding photo, the starboard side of *Enterprise* was photographed from aft. A mobile crane and its tractor, part of the essential equipment of a Navy carrier, are spotted on the aft end of the flight deck. Midway between that crane and the island, a civilian woodie station wagon is parked.

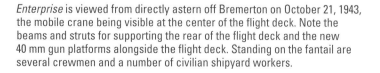

Enterprise is viewed from directly astern off Bremerton on October 21, 1943, the mobile crane being visible at the center of the flight deck. Note the beams and struts for supporting the rear of the flight deck and the new 40 mm gun platforms alongside the flight deck. Standing on the fantail are several crewmen and a number of civilian shipyard workers.

In a bow-on view of *Enterprise* on October 21, 1943, a twin 40 mm antiaircraft gun mount has been installed on the platform with a splinter shield above the forecastle. On the starboard side of that platform is a raised tub containing the director for that 40 mm gun mount. Below each side of the forward end of the flight deck are newly installed twin 40 mm gun mounts on platforms with splinter shields.

The newly refurbished *Enterprise* is underway off Dungeness Point, Washington, on November 1, 1943, at a speed of 23 knots. After departing from Puget Sound, the ship would sail to Pearl Harbor.

The *Enterprise* is viewed from the starboard side off Dungeness Point on November 1, 1943, at a speed of 23 knots. The aft roller curtains of the hangar deck are raised, allowing a view through the hangar and what appears to be a boat stored inside it.

USS ENTERPRISE (CV6)
Off Dungeness Point
1 November 1943
Speed 23 knots
Astern
Stl. #8528

USS ENTERPRISE (CV6)
Off Dungeness Point
1 November 1943
Speed 23 knots
Head on
Stl. #8524

Still making 23 knots, *Enterprise* is viewed from astern as it steams past Dungeness Point on its voyage toward Pearl Harbor. The largest guns on the carrier would remain the eight single 5-inch/38-caliber pieces.

A final aerial photo of *Enterprise* departing from Puget Sound on November 1, 1943, shows the carrier from the front. Its next combat would be in the invasion of Tarawa, later that month, and by that time the *Enterprise* would be equipped with a force of night fighters.

During flight operations against Japanese forces on Makin Island, in the Gilbert Islands, on November 10, 1943, Ens. Byron M. Johnson of VF-2 crashed his F6F, no. 30, on the flight deck of the *Enterprise*. Here, Lt. Walter L. Chewning, the catapult officer, is climbing up to the wing to help Ens. Johnson escape the flames. Johnson was able to escape with minimal injuries.

Firefighters are spraying Ens. Johnson's F6F Hellcat after the crash on the flight deck on November 10, 1943. After this photo was taken, the plane was pushed over the side.

On Christmas Day 1943, a dive-bomber and six torpedo bombers landed on USS *Enterprise* bearing Christmas gifts for the crew. In the passenger's seat of the jeep is Lt. Louis L. Bangs, of Air Group 10, who portrayed Santa Claus. The planes were marked with the names of Santa's reindeer; in the background is a TBF/TBM Avenger torpedo bomber with the name "Vexen" (i.e., Vixen) painted on the cowling.

Mess cooks in the *Enterprise* are preparing to carve roasted turkeys in preparation for a Christmas feast, December 15, 1943.

RAdm. J. W. Reeves, left foreground, commander of the *Enterprise*'s Task Group 58.1, observes from a bridge on *Enterprise* as a Grumman Hellcat from VF-10 launches from the starboard catapult as two other Hellcats, numbers 61 and 19, prepare to take off on a mission during January 1944. The Hellcats are painted in tricolor camouflage: Sea Blue, Intermediate Blue, and Insignia White.

In a photo probably taken on the same occasion as the preceding one, RAdm. Reeves, seated to the left, confers with staff officers on a bridge on *Enterprise*. On the forward bulkhead next to the talker to the left is a chart listing the numbers of planes launched by the carriers *Enterprise*, *Yorktown* (CV-10), *Belleau Wood* (CVL-24), and *Cowpens* (CVL-25).

With Grumman F6F Hellcats spotted on the flight deck, a Vought F4U-2 Corsair night fighter is descending on elevator no. 2 to the hangar deck of USS *Enterprise* on January 20, 1944. The F4U-2 was an experimental conversion of the F4U-1, being equipped with an airborne-intercept radar in a radome on the right wing. Five .50-caliber machine guns were mounted: three in the left wing and two in the right. Some of the F4U-2s served with VF(N)-101 aboard USS *Enterprise* and USS *Intrepid* in early 1944.

A photographer in a passing aircraft snapped this photo above the bow of the *Enterprise* while it was en route to an attack on the Japanese airbase at Taroa Island, Maloelap Atoll, in the Marshall Islands, on January 22, 1944. Scattered individuals are walking around or relaxing on the flight deck.

During the advance to the Marshall Islands on January 22, 1944, the *Enterprise* crossed the equator, an occasion that called for a Neptune party. This party is one of the ancient rites of mariners and is an initiation of seamen and officers as well as enlisted men who are crossing the equator for the first time. Here, three members of King Neptune's court are keeping a lookout for the equator, ready to report the sighting to the ship's captain as soon as they spot it.

In the foreground, crewmen of the *Enterprise* are enjoying their first meals as newly rated chief petty officers (CPOs) by eating from wooden troughs, using giant forks and 16-inch carving knives: a ritual that, according to the original inscription on the photo, was considered a "proper induction into their new rate."

Members of the crew of the *Enterprise* look on as three crewmen of a TBF/TBM Avenger bob to the surface after their plane crashed upon takeoff from the carrier. The incident occurred on January 21, 1944, during operations against Japanese forces in the Marshall Islands. The three men subsequently were rescued by a destroyer escorting the *Enterprise*.

On the hangar deck of USS *Enterprise* while it was anchored at Majuro, in the Marshall Islands, on February 27, with Lt. Horace I. Proulx (*right*), refereeing, five African American stewards are engaged in a blindfolded boxing match for the amusement of the crew. Until the US military services were integrated following World War II, African Americans serving in the Navy were relegated chiefly to mess attendants and cooks.

During a weeklong layover at Majuro, in the Marshall Islands, on April 10, 1944, members of the *Enterprise*'s Construction and Repair Department are making repairs to the flight deck under the cover of a shelter made of lumber and canvas. The C&R Department found that its members could work around the clock in fair and foul weather using this portable shelter.

Deck crewmen of the *Enterprise* are using a mobile crane to recover an F6F Hellcat that turned over on the flight deck after crashing into the barrier during a landing off Hollandia, New Guinea, on April 18, 1944. This was during preinvasion operations for Operation Reckless, the US invasion of Hollandia. The pilot of the Hellcat, Lt. (j.g.) George Carrington, suffered only minor injuries in the crash.

A photographer on the rear of the island of the *Enterprise* captured this view of a Grumman Hellcat fighter on elevator no. 2, *foreground*, while Avenger torpedo bombers warm their engine in the background. Crewmen are leaning on a safety rail around the elevator well; when the elevator platform moved below the level of the main deck, this rail was elevated to the position seen here. A jeep is parked on the flight deck to the far left. At this time the *Enterprise* was allocated four such vehicles which were used as light aircraft tugs.

After providing air support for the invasion of Saipan, *Enterprise* steered for Pearl Harbor. While in Pearl Harbor in July 1944, *Enterprise* got a new captain, Capt. Cato D. Glover Jr., and was assigned new fliers, Air Group 20, which replaced Air Group 10. At the same time, the faithful Douglas SBD Dauntlesses left the ship, replaced by much larger, and much less liked, Curtiss SB2C-3 Helldivers. During the monthlong stay at Pearl, the ship was repainted in Measure 33 patter 4Ab camouflage, a dazzle pattern.

Repainted, reequipped, and rearmed, *Enterprise* sailed on August 16 for Eniwetok, where US forces were staging for an assault on the Bonin Islands. Three days of attacks on Chichijima began on August 31, 1944, after which *Enterprise* and its consorts in Task Group 38.4 moved to attack Yap in the Carolines, beginning on September 6, for the first time using napalm.

The task group then moved on to the Palau islands, where they began their raids on September 10. Five days later the landings began on Peleliu, the most famous of the Palaus. The carriers continued to provide support for the Marines landing through the seventeenth.

Leaving the Palaus, *Enterprise* steamed toward Manus in the Admiralty Islands and, in doing so, crossed the equator southbound. With the US Navy essentially controlling the sea by this time, the crew was allowed a bit of humor and frivolity through a traditional Neptune party. At Manus, the crew enjoyed three days of rest and relaxation, as best that could be had on primitive beaches.

In October, Halsey moved against Okinawa, taking with him Task Force 38, which by this time boasted seventeen fast carriers, six battleships, fourteen cruisers, sixty destroyers, and numerous support vessels. On October 10, *Enterprise*'s Hellcats strafed an unsuspecting Japanese airfield on Okinawa, destroying many enemy planes on the ground. This was followed by the Helldivers sinking four transports and an escort off Naha Town.

On October 12, the carriers attacked Formosa (Taiwan), with Fighting 20 claiming twenty-one kills in the first raid. The carriers spent three days attacking targets in, around, and above Formosa.

Three days later *Enterprise* and its aviators turned their attention to the Philippines. The Philippines were critically important to Japan, both due to their proximity and because of the islands' position relative to the petroleum-shipping route from the East Indies. Accordingly, the islands were well defended. Over three days, aircraft from the *Enterprise* bombed targets, often airfields, and faced off against Japanese pilots. When *Enterprise* moved on, its fliers had downed sixty-nine enemy airplanes, losing twenty-two of their own in the process.

The task group began withdrawing toward Ulithi for rest, but that plan changed on October 21, when it was learned that the Japanese fleet was again at sea in force. The Japanese strategy was a three-prong attack, with two prongs striking the American amphibious force in the Leyte Gulf while the third group, including Japan's four remaining carriers, would lure the US carriers to the north so the Allied aircraft could not defend the amphibious force.

On October 24, *Enterprise* scouts located a Japanese force including two battleships, a cruiser, and seven destroyers. The large scouting force of *Enterprise* aircraft collected over the ships and began their attacks at the battleships. Incredibly, the Japanese used the 14-inch main batteries of the battlewagons as antiaircraft guns.

Half of the aviators attacked the lead battleship, the *Yamashiro*, with the others attacking the trailing battleship, the *Fusō*. Rocket-armed Hellcats led the Helldivers, armed with only a pair of 500-pound bombs due to the range, after the ships, the fighters' machine guns and rockets suppressing antiaircraft fire. A few of the aircraft attacked the cruiser *Mogami*, a veteran of previous attacks by *Enterprise* airmen.

Early the next day, scouts from the *Intrepid* found another Japanese force. At that time, *Enterprise* was readying a deckload strike force, which seized the opportunity presented by *Intrepid*'s find, and launched the strike at 1315. They arrived over the Japanese ships at 1500, among which the standout target was the *Musashi*, the world's largest battleship.

Enterprise's men put bombs, rockets, and torpedoes into the battleship and were soon joined by fliers from *Franklin*, *Intrepid*, and *Cabot*, sealing the battleship's fate. *Musashi* went down at 1936.

On the twenty-fifth, the Japanese northern force, which included the four carriers, was spotted 120 miles away. As the Japanese had anticipated, Halsey launched against them. *Enterprise* planned four strikes: two in the morning, one midday, and one in the late afternoon. They were joined by aircraft from the other US carriers, and before the day was over, all four of the Japanese carriers had disappeared beneath the Pacific waves in what came to be known as the Battle of Leyte Gulf.

On October 30 *Enterprise* was attacked by a new weapon; the kamikaze. Although one hit near enough the debris landed aboard, the three that attacked the Big E failed to hit it. Other carriers were not so fortunate, since both *Franklin* and *Belleau Wood* took hits.

The damage to the *Franklin* was such that RAdm. Davison and his staff transferred his flag to *Enterprise*.

On November 11, *Enterprise* aviators attacked Japanese ships in Ormoc Bay, sinking two destroyers and a cargo ship. For ten days *Enterprise* roamed off the Philippines, striking various targets and losing an Avenger crew and five fighter pilots in the process. At Ulithi, Air Group 20 was transferred to *Lexington*, while *Lexington*'s Air Group 19 came aboard *Enterprise* for a ride back to Pearl Harbor. When Air Group 20 left *Enterprise*, it had racked up a tally of 135 enemy planes downed. *Enterprise* pulled into Pearl Harbor on December 6.

When it left port on Christmas Eve 1944, under command of Capt. Grover B. H. Hall, it had a new mission. The veteran carrier had been redesignated as a night carrier, the first full-size fleet carrier to be so classified.

Enterprise's first action in its new role occurred on January 7, 1945, when a night raid was launched against Clark Field, Manila. *Enterprise*'s radar-equipped Hellcats downed various Japanese night fliers, while its bombers attacked Japanese airfields.

January 12 found *Enterprise* in the South China Sea, its aircraft scouring the Tonkin Gulf looking for Japanese battleships that had erroneously been reported to be in the area. They did, however, find a Japanese coastal convoy, which they attacked, sinking one freighter and badly damaging two more.

Over January 16–17, Task Force 38 attacked Japanese positions on the China coast, with *Enterprise* contributing to the night operations. Big E lost five aircraft and two pilots during the operation, with nothing to show for it.

The following week, *Enterprise* was off Formosa. A nighttime eight-plane attack on vessels in Kiirun Harbor was launched on January 22. Japanese radar plotted the arrival of the American airplanes, relaying the information to flak and searchlight batteries. Although the raid claimed a small ship and ignited some fires ashore, it had cost three well-trained Avenger crews.

Retiring toward Ulithi, *Enterprise* lost another flier in an attack on Okinawa. The carrier spent two weeks in the safe anchorage of Ulithi, giving the men a well-deserved rest and the carrier some needed maintenance.

On January 26, *Enterprise* sailed from Ulithi, joining Task Force 58 as the carrier moved against the Japanese home islands for the first time since the Doolittle Raid almost three years prior. *Enterprise* was not alone in the night carrier duties, since *Saratoga* had joined in, replacing the light carrier *Independence* in the role.

On February 16–17, the men from the *Enterprise* struck airfields on Honshu, especially those around Tokyo. These raids were intended primarily as diversions masking the actual thrust—Iwo Jima—600 miles to the south.

Enterprise and *Saratoga* arrived off Iwo Jima on February 19, beginning operations there in support of the Marines going ashore. On the twenty-first, *Saratoga* sustained five bomb hits and three kamikaze hits, forcing it back to Bremerton for repair, leaving *Enterprise* as the solo night carrier.

When most of Task Force 58 left Iwo on February 23 to again strike Honshu, *Enterprise* remained behind. For the next seven days and six hours—174 hours total—*Enterprise* sustained continuous around-the-clock air operations. Severe weather forced the stoppage of air operations on March 2, but they resumed the next day and continued until March 9.

Following a brief respite at Ulithi, on March 14 *Enterprise* steamed again toward Japan. On the night of the eighteenth, *Enterprise* night fliers began harassing the enemy airfields and radar sites. By the nineteenth the fighters from the *Enterprise* had also downed four enemy aircraft at night, and remarkably over the next two days, night Avengers from the ship also downed two more Japanese aircraft, with a third listed as a "probable."

However, the American carriers, so close to Japan, were prime targets as well. On the eighteenth a Japanese bomb landed on the deck of the *Enterprise*, thankfully failing to detonate. The crew tossed it overboard.

During an overhaul at Pearl Harbor between July 16 and August 3, 1944, USS *Enterprise* was repainted in Measure 33 (Variant 4AB) camouflage, a dazzle pattern that, according to official plans specific to *Enterprise*, consisted of Haze Gray (5-H), Pale Gray (5-P), and Ocean Gray (5-O) paint on the vertical surfaces; Deck Blue (20-B) paint on horizontal metal surfaces; and Deck Blue Stain 21 on the wooden flight deck. The *Enterprise* is seen here off Pearl Harbor in the new camouflage on August 2, 1944. *US Navy*

Enterprise went to General Quarters 0513 on March 19, an hour before the sun rose, as a precaution called for by Capt. Hall, and not without reason. Shortly thereafter the new *Wasp* was hit, with 100 men killed. In quick succession the *Franklin*, not at General Quarters, was hit as well, costing 800 men their lives.

On the twentieth, *Enterprise* was targeted by a Japanese bomber, whose bomb landed 50 feet from the hull, causing minimal concussive damage. Worse though was the damage and death caused by overzealous gunners of escort ships, who put 5-inch rounds close above the carrier, the shrapnel cutting down *Enterprise*'s men and setting six fueled Hellcats ablaze. The spreading gasoline fire from the F6Fs cooked off machine gun and antiaircraft ammunition, forcing the damage control parties to retreat. The spreading smoke and flames forced the Combat Information Center (CIC) and radio and flight control stations to be abandoned in favor of backup stations deeper in the ship. The fire burned through the fir flight deck to the hanger below, but the sprinklers were triggered by damage control personnel, preventing the blaze from gaining a foothold in the hangar.

Capt. Hall swung the ship so that the prevailing wind would push the smoke away, allowing damage control parties better access; thus they extinguished the topside flames in less that an hour.

Enterprise withdrew to Ulithi, where the ship's force joined the men of the repair ship *Jason* in erasing the damage. Men not involved in the ten-day repair were able to enjoy some time ashore.

Repairs complete, *Enterprise*, as night carrier, sailed on April 5 to join *Intrepid*, *Yorktown*, and *Langley* in Operation Iceberg off Okinawa. With Task Force 58 operating in relatively confined waters, so close to Japanese shore installations, the ships became prime targets for the suicide-bent kamikaze pilots. On April 6, 350 attacked, sinking three ships. Over the next six weeks another 368 Allied ships were damaged and thirty-three were sunk. *Enterprise* was again wounded on April 11. A morning suicide attack was narrowly thwarted, and an afternoon near-miss by a kamikaze buckled some hull plating and caused an assortment of other light damage. Worse, one man was killed and eighteen wounded.

Withdrawing again to Ulithi for repair, *Jason*'s men toiled for over two weeks returning *Enterprise* to shipshape condition. Repairs complete, on May 3 *Enterprise* steamed again toward Okinawa. *Enterprise* was operating with Task Group 58.3, which included Task Force flagship *Bunker Hill*, on May 11. On that morning, two kamikaze hit *Bunker Hill* within thirty seconds of each other, engulfing the carrier in flames and killing 346 men, with a further forty-three missing. Well over 200 more men were injured. Vice Admiral Marc Mitscher relocated his flag to *Enterprise*.

Wearing its new Measure 33 (Variant 4AB) dazzle camouflage, the *Enterprise* is viewed off its starboard beam off Oahu on August 2, 1944.

The Big E's nocturnal aircraft struck targets in Kyushu on May 11 and 12. Essentially unopposed on the eleventh, the next night searchlights and flak were ready but the fliers pressed on. Elsewhere that night, *Enterprise* fighters tangled with a variety of Japanese aircraft, downing eight of the enemy with no casualties among the Navy men.

As the sun rose on the morning of May 14, *Enterprise*'s night fighters were returning home, having downed three more enemy aircraft. Aboard *Enterprise*, radar operators detected a large flight of inbound enemy aircraft at various altitudes, twenty-six in all.

The inbound Hellcats were alerted, as were those of other ships, and soon thereafter the number of Japanese was reduced to ten. Antiaircraft gunners claimed six more, three turned away, but one bore on, darting in and out of cloud cover. At 0657, that plane, piloted by Lt. Shunsuke Tomiyasu, plunged toward the *Enterprise*. Capt. Hall swung hard port, hoping not only to evade the kamikaze but also allowing more antiaircraft guns to be brought to bear. At 200 yards out, Tomiyasu corrected, rolled the fighter onto its back, and plunged into *Enterprise*'s deck, hitting just aft of the no. 1 elevator. The blast hurled much of the 15-ton elevator 400 feet into the air.

Damage control and medical parties rushed into action, entering an aviation-gas-fueled inferno to retrieve the wounded, toss ammunition overboard, and push back the flames. In seventeen minutes the fire had been brought under control, and two hours later it was out. While all life is precious, *Enterprise*'s casualties were light compared to other stricken carriers, or even its own from past engagements: fourteen men, including three officers, were dead, and about sixty were wounded, half seriously. *Enterprise* buried its dead at sea, including Tomiyasu, whose body was recovered from the remains of his Zeke in the elevator well. He too was given an honorable burial at sea.

On the morning of the fifteenth, Mitscher again transferred his flag, this time to the carrier *Randolph*. The next day, *Enterprise*, unable to launch or recover planes, steamed first for Ulithi, then to Pearl Harbor, where it arrived to a hero's welcome on May 30. Two days later it sailed for Bremerton, streaming a 578-foot-long homeward-bound pennant, one foot for each day since leaving Bremerton on November 1, 1943.

Five days and 2,645 miles later, *Enterprise* entered Puget Sound Navy Yard. *Enterprise* was there being brought back into fighting condition when the Japanese surrendered. At last, the war was over, but the *Enterprise*'s service was not.

Wearing its new Measure 33 (Variant 4AB) dazzle camouflage, the *Enterprise* is viewed off its port beam off Oahu on August 2, 1944.

An aerial photographer captured this view of *Enterprise* low off its port stern on August 2, 1944. Groups of crewmen are assembled at various places on the flight deck. *US Navy*

In another aerial view of USS *Enterprise* off Oahu on August 2, 1944, the carrier's number, "6," is faintly visible on the fore and aft ends of the flight deck, in a slightly darker tone than the rest of the deck.

The demarcation between the Navy Blue (port side) and Haze Gray (starboard) on the stern of the *Enterprise* is apparent in this August 2, 1944, aerial photo. The Navy Blue and Haze Gray pattern continues on the ramp on the rear of the flight deck.

The layout of the markings on the flight deck is evident. Both of the carrier's number "6"s on the flight deck are oriented the same way, with their bottoms toward the aft.

As seen in a frontal aerial view of *Enterprise* on October 2, 1944, the ramp on the forward end of the flight deck was painted Haze Gray (the lighter color) and Navy Blue.

Enterprise is viewed from above, off its port bow, in this final photo of the series taken on October 2, 1944, exhibiting some of the three-color patterns on the vertical surfaces on the port side. *National Museum of Naval Aviation*

USS *Enterprise* is at sea with its air group embarked, in or around August 1944, with fresh-appearing Measure 33 (Variant 4AB) dazzle camouflage paint. Most of the aircraft are painted in the late-war camouflage scheme of overall Glossy Sea Blue, while a number of Curtiss SB2C Helldivers on the aft part of the flight deck are in three-color camouflage. Light-colored triangle unit markings are on the vertical tails, with the aircraft numbers marked on them. *National Museum of Naval Aviation*

Several scoreboards to highlight the exploits of *Enterprise*'s air groups were painted on the outboard bulkhead of the quarterdeck area of the hangar deck. The one depicted in this photograph dated August 20, 1944, recounted the operations against Japanese forces in the Pacific from November 15, 1942, to the Battle of the Philippine Sea, in June 1944, listing dates, actions, and Japanese losses in ships sunk and damaged, aircraft destroyed, and shore installations destroyed. Below this chart is another one listing the carrier's air groups, with space reserved for Air Group 20.

During the Battle of Surigao Strait, part of the Battle of Leyte Gulf, at 0908 on the morning of October 24, 1944, aircraft from the *Enterprise* spotted and attacked the Fusō-class dreadnought battleship *Yamashiro*, subjecting the ship to bombing, strafing, and a barrage of aerial rockets. A near miss by a bomb caused a rupture in the hull. Later that day, US Navy surface ships finished off the ship. In this photo, bombs have exploded to each side, one to starboard and three to port, sending up columns of water.

A photographer aboard the Essex-class aircraft carrier *Ticonderoga* (CV-14) took this image of USS *Enterprise* at anchor with its air group embarked at Ulithi Atoll on January 25, 1945. The carrier remained at that harbor until the end of the month, before joining Task Group 58.5 in early February on a raid against Honshu, Japan. Just ahead of the island there is what appears to be a 2½-ton 6×6 truck outfitted as a weather station.

A General Motors TBM Avenger skids along the flight deck of the *Enterprise* following right main landing-gear failure upon landing, during airstrikes against southern Japan on March 7, 1945. The plane was equipped with a radome on the leading edge of the right wing, as well as Yagi radar antennas on the tops of the wings. Two of the propeller blade tips were chipped in the crash.

As the Japanese aircraft approached the *Enterprise* early on the morning of March 18, 1945, it dropped a bomb, which struck the forward elevator, but because of the plane's proximity and shallow angle of attack, the bomb ricocheted off the elevator without detonating, striking the structural supports for the navigating bridge before crashing without exploding onto the fight deck. In this March 20, 1945, photo, taken after the attack, a crewmen is chopping away damaged planking on elevator no. 1.

Slightly after 0730 on the morning of March 18, 1945, while USS *Enterprise* was conducting operations against the Japanese home islands, a single Japanese airplane made a head-on attack on the carrier. Gunners on the carrier and its escorts initially mistook the plane for a Grumman Wildcat, allowing it to approach quite near before coming under antiaircraft fire. In this photo, the antiaircraft guns of *Enterprise* and its escorts are fully engaged against the incoming Japanese aircraft.

The path of the Japanese dud bomb crashed it into the lower forward-port quarter of the navigating bridge and then punched its way through several of the steel support brackets for the bridge and Pri Fly. Note the shattered window in the Pri Fly wing bridge, and the fact that the island is painted in a single color: the dazzle camouflage had been replaced by Measure 21 camouflage, with Navy Blue on vertical surfaces, in December 1944.

If the *Enterprise* escaped serious damage in the attack of March 18, 1945, its luck was not so good two days later. On March 20, the task group came under repeated harassing attacks by Japanese aircraft, flying singly or in small groups. One bomb missed the carrier by 50 feet, and another near miss disabled the starboard steering machinery. *Enterprise* is seen from a distance during an attack on March 20, 1945, with flak bursts from the carrier and its escorts in the sky above.

At the same time the near miss knocked out the *Enterprise*'s starboard steering machinery, the carrier fell victim to a "friendly-fire" incident of disastrous dimensions. Gunners in escort ships, in their attempt to shoot down the Japanese plane that dropped the bomb, inadvertently fired two 5-inch projectiles that burst to the front of the *Enterprise*'s island. One shell exploded near the quadruple 40 mm gun mounts to the front of the island, killing and wounding many crewmen of those mounts and setting fire to fueled-up Hellcats on the flight deck. The other 5-inch shell exploded off the port bow, causing further damage to the carrier. This photo, taken from the carrier USS *Hancock* (CV-19), shows the conflagration and billowing smoke created by the friendly-fire incident.

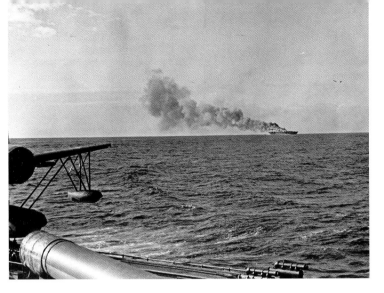

Flames and smoke pour from the flight deck of *Enterprise* after the friendly-fire incident of March 20, 1945. The photo was taken from the aft main deck of an unidentified ship in *Enterprise*'s task group; to the left is a Vought OS2U Kingfisher floatplane on a catapult.

As the flames are spreading among the Hellcats spotted on the forward end of the flight deck of *Enterprise* following the friendly-fire incident on March 20, 1944, firefighters are spraying firefighting foam on the planes. This was a perilous time for the carrier: an out-of-control fire on the flight deck could cripple or destroy the ship.

With flames spread across the deck, licking the belly tanks of the Hellcats, a damage control team advances, attempting to snuff out the flames.

Firefighters continue to combat the flames on the flight deck on March 20, 1945, by laying down firefighting foam and a fog of sprayed water. Even as these men continued in their valiant efforts to save the ship, they were imperiled by exploding ammunition, flying fragments, and continuing attempts by the enemy to dive-bomb the carrier. Burning magnesium on the wheels of parked aircraft posed a particular problem, but all fires on the flight deck were extinguished within thirty-five minutes, and electrical fires in the island were put out within fifty minutes.

Firefighting foam, also called mechanical foam, is slathered over much of the flight deck forward of the quadruple 40 mm gun mounts to the front of the island of USS *Enterprise* as firefighters conclude their successful efforts to stanch the fire on the deck on March 20, 1945. In the foreground is a mobile crane.

In a photo taken from the port side of the island following the friendly-fire incident on March 20, 1944, crewmen slosh through firefighting foam as they clear the flight deck of debris after the flames have been extinguished. Fires destroyed Pri Fly (*upper right*) and the port signal bridge on the island. On the flight deck below Pri Fly are the remains of a burned-out Hellcat, while the remnants of two engine assemblies lie on the deck toward the center of the photo.

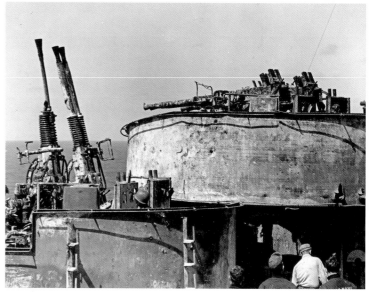

Firefighters combat the flames set off by fuel from Grumman F6F Hellcats on the flight deck of *Enterprise* on March 20, 1945. At times, the fires threatened to burn through the flight deck, endangering the planes on the hangar deck below. This photo provides another view of the damage to the navigating bridge caused by a Japanese dud bomb two days earlier, on March 18.

The two quadruple 40 mm gun mounts to the front of the carrier's island (40 mm mounts nos. 5 and 7) and their crews came in for particular devastation from the explosion of a US 5-inch shell and the resulting gasoline fire on March 20, 1945. Of the crews of these two mounts, eight were killed and twenty-two were wounded. The photo was taken on March 20.

The *Enterprise* came under kamikaze attack off Okinawa on April 11, 1945, when two suicide planes, each carrying a 250-kilogram bomb, attempted to crash into the carrier. At around 1408 in the afternoon, the first plane plowed into the sponsons of 40 mm gun mounts nos. 8 and 10, on the port side near frame 136, before crashing into the sea. The engine of that plane, torn from its mounting, punched a hole in the port blister, while the bomb on that plane exploded underwater at around frame 134, causing further damage to the hull. A photographer amidships on the *Enterprise* snapped this photo at the moment the first plane crashed into the ship. Less than an hour later, at 1500, a second Japanese suicide plane attempted to crash on the *Enterprise* but missed, slamming into the ocean some 50 feet off the starboard bow opposite frame 30. The detonation of the bomb on this plane caused further structural and shock damage to the ship, including setting a plane on the flight deck on fire. The flames were extinguished before they spread very far.

Firefighters are putting out flames on the flight deck with firefighting foam after the Japanese suicide attack on *Enterprise* on April 11, 1945. Toward the rear of the starboard catapult, firefighters are concentrating foam on the severed tail section of an F6F Hellcat. This evidently was the remnant of a Hellcat that was poised for takeoff on that catapult at the time of the suicide attack, and which caught fire. The flaming fighter plane was catapulted off the deck in order to get rid of the danger it posed.

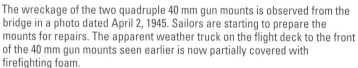

The wreckage of the two quadruple 40 mm gun mounts is observed from the bridge in a photo dated April 2, 1945. Sailors are starting to prepare the mounts for repairs. The apparent weather truck on the flight deck to the front of the 40 mm gun mounts seen earlier is now partially covered with firefighting foam.

Damage from the first kamikaze plane to crash into *Enterprise* on April 11, 1945, is seen eleven days later, on April 22, 1945. Some of the damage to 40 mm gun mounts nos. 8 and 10 has been repaired in the field, and the guns are loaded and manned. Permanent repairs would be made soon at Ulithi. The damaged parts of the splinter shields and platforms had been cut away. Severed gasoline drain lines are protruding from the side of the hull.

The *Enterprise* was on the receiving end of many Japanese attacks during World War II, but the one that finally put it out of the war came on the morning of May 14, 1945, southeast of the Japanese home island of Kyushu. Lt. (j.g.) Shunsuke Tomiyasu, flying an A6M5 "Zeke" carrying a 500-kilogram bomb with a delayed-action fuse, managed to slip through Task Force 58's combat air patrol. As Tomiyasu came in at high speed toward the *Enterprise*, he executed a snap roll at the last moment, shown here, before crashing into the forward part of the flight deck.

Lt. (j.g.) Shunsuke Tomiyasu crashed his Zeke into the flight deck of *Enterprise*, just aft of elevator no. 1, at 0657. The bomb traveled several decks below, and its explosion blew elevator 1 some 400 feet into the sky. Shown here is the explosion, with the elevator platform at the top of the smoke plume. This image was taken by a photographer aboard the light aircraft carrier USS *Bataan* (CVL-29).

As photographed from the front of the island of *Enterprise*, smoke pours out of the elevator well as firefighters work to put out the fires. Just aft of the elevator opening, smoke obscures the hole in the flight deck where Tomiyasu's Zeke crashed through.

A firefighting crew continues to douse the flames in the well of elevator no. 1 in the aftermath of the May 14, 1945, suicide attack. Teetering precariously near the forward-port corner of the well is the remnant of a F6F Hellcat; another Hellcat, with wings folded, is at the front of the flight deck. In this attack, thirteen crewmen were killed and sixty-eight were wounded.

Once the smoke had subsided, a photographer on the *Enterprise* took this view from the hangar deck down into the well of elevator no. 1, showing remnants of the elevator beams and the devastation below. A number of crewmen are on the second deck, several of whom are gathered around the hole in the deck where the Zeke and its bomb crashed through to the third deck. Fortunately, bales of rags and a quantity of steel plates were stored in the lower part of the elevator well, and these materials cushioned some of the effects of the kamikaze plane, preventing even greater devastation. Within seventeen minutes of the suicide attack, the fires on the ship were under control; thirteen minutes later, all fires had been extinguished.

This is the hole in the flight deck, around frame 42, where the Zeke suicide plane crashed through it. The view is facing aft and to port. The blast bowed the flight deck and its support trusses upward, to a maximum of around 3 feet.

Unable to deploy, launch, or land aircraft, *Enterprise* retired, first to Ulithi to unload bombs and ammunition, then to Pearl Harbor, and finally to Puget Sound Navy Yard, Bremerton, Washington, for repairs. This photo of the well of elevator no. 1 with the debris removed was taken at Bremerton; the orientation is to the port and forward. The steel plates of the bulkheads were dished from the blast and had many punctures from flying fragments.

This view from the hangar deck aft of the well of elevator no. 1, looking forward and to port, shows the bowed overhead trusses and flight deck. Frame 54 is at the top, and bulkhead 26, which formed the forward partition of the elevator well above the hangar deck, is in the background in the lower right.

USS *Enterprise* underwent extensive repairs at Puget Sound Navy Yard from June 12 to August 31, 1945, and thus was inactive during the end of the war in the Pacific. The carrier is seen here departing from Puget Sound, Washington, on September 13, 1945.

U.S.S. Enterprise
CV-6
Broad on Stbd. Quarter
Puget Sound, Wn.

Enterprise is viewed from off its starboard stern on September 13, 1945. Recent work at Bremerton included the installation of four Mk. 57 directors with Mk. 28 Mod. 2 radar, and the installation of radar antennas on four of the 40 mm gun mounts. Dish antennas are visible on two of the 40 mm mounts: the raised mount to the immediate front of the island, and the second mount aft of the island. *US Navy*

CV-6
Broad on Port Quarter
Puget Sound, Wn.
Speed 20 Knots

This final photo of USS *Enterprise* departing from Puget Sound on September 13, 1945, was taken above its aft-port beam. Two whip antennas are lowered along the flight deck, opposite the front of the island. Nests of life rafts are secured to the bulkheads along the hangar deck at various places.

CHAPTER 8
Navy Day, Magic Carpet, and the End of the "Big E"

With World War II concluded, in late September 1945, the *Enterprise* began the final phase of its operational career, as a transport ship for Operation Magic Carpet: the mass movement of GIs from the theaters of war back to the United States, by ships and aircraft. *Enterprise* brought its first consignment of Magic Carpet servicemen from Pearl Harbor to New York via the Panama Canal. The carrier is seen here transiting the Miraflores Locks in the canal alongside the battleship USS *Washington* (BB-56), which is in the foreground, on October 12, 1945. *Enterprise* arrived with its passengers at New York on October 17, 1945.

Its repairs complete, and with its antiaircraft suite upgraded yet again, *Enterprise* left Bremerton bound for Pearl Harbor via San Francisco on September 13, arriving in Hawaii on September 23.

There it brought aboard its new Night Air Group 55; a new captain, Capt. William Rees; and VAdm. Frederick C. Sherman. Also coming aboard were 1,149 former POWs and released hospital patients bound for the mainland and discharge. It sailed from Pearl Harbor the last time on September 25, bound not for the West Coast but for New York City.

This sailing, on which it was joined by the light carriers *Monterey* and *Bataan*, as well as four battleships, was the first of what would be four "Magic Carpet" trips returning service men home. On October 11, *Enterprise* entered the west end of the Panama Canal and began passing through into waters that it had not felt since April 1939.

In the morning of October 17, *Enterprise* was entering New York harbor, where at 0720 it would tie up at Pier 26 in the North River. Over the next two weeks it received 300,000 visitors. The next day, when speaking to reporters aboard, Admiral Sherman acknowledged that there was about to be a massive drawdown in the Navy that would likely render the *Enterprise* surplus, and he opined that "she might well be preserved as a historical museum, I favor that."

While welcoming guests, *Enterprise*'s crew made ready for the upcoming official Navy Day celebration and the review by President Harry Truman. *Enterprise*'s band led the victory parade down the Avenue of the Americas. The Navy Day celebration ended with the dusk flyover of Night Air Group 55; their aircraft, with lights turned on, first flew over in a "V" for victory formation, then in an "E" for *Enterprise* formation. On October 31, *Enterprise* steamed the relatively short distance to the Boston Navy Yard,

where laborers filled its cavernous hanger with bunks. The wells of the fore and aft elevators were filled with heads (toilets). While hardly luxurious, *Enterprise* became a voluminous transport to return troops to the US from Europe.

The day after *Enterprise* entered the Boston Navy Yard, Secretary of the Navy James Forrestal wrote to President Truman, saying that the time had come to withdraw *Enterprise* from service since modern aircraft had outgrown it, and urging that the ship "should be returned permanently to some proper place as a visible symbol of American valor and tenacity in war."

But for now, there were troops to bring home. Arriving in Southampton to take aboard troops, on November 23, First Sea Lord, Sir Albert Alexander, led an Admiralty delegation aboard the ship. During that visit, Mrs. Alexander presented the Admiralty pennant, then flying above the ship and marking the presence of the board, to the *Enterprise*, saying, "The board of the Admiralty would be proud if you would accept the gift of this flat to *Enterprise* as a token of respect for her gallant record and as a sincere tribute from a great and historic navy to the prowess of the comrade in arms in the United States fleet."

A few days later it sailed for the United States with 4,668 servicemen aboard.

Tugboats are assisting USS *Enterprise* into position off Manhattan on October 17, 1945. The carrier was visiting the city for Navy Day celebrations, during which *Enterprise* would render a twenty-one-gun salute to President Harry S. Truman.

Sailors aboard the light carrier USS *Monterey* (CVL-26) watch as tugboats maneuver the carrier *Enterprise* to Pier 26, on the west side of Manhattan, on October 17, 1945. Several aircraft with wings folded, including TBF/TBM Avengers, are spotted on the flight deck of the *Enterprise*. On the far left of the pier are Red Cross workers who will welcome the personnel disembarking from the *Enterprise*, dispensing donuts, coffee, and fresh milk. *Hampton Roads Naval Museum*

On December 13, *Enterprise* sailed from England for the second and final time, battling four North Atlantic storms to reach Bayonne, New Jersey, on Christmas Eve, dashing hopes of its 4,413 passengers and crew to be truly home for Christmas. The passengers were discharged, and some of the crew were granted liberty.

Early on Christmas morning, *Enterprise*'s chaplain's office got a call from the administrator of a nearby boy's orphanage, advising that there was no chance of providing a "Merry Christmas" to the 140 children there, not even a special Christmas meal, and asking for help. All hands were rousted, the ship prepared for visitors, cooks prepared additional Christmas dinners, a Christmas tree was erected, and some crew fashioned toys. *Enterprise*'s men, missing their own families and home life, did the best they could to spoil the children.

On New Years Day 1946, *Enterprise* stood out for the Azores, returning sixteen days later with 3,345 men and 212 WACs from San Miguel. When it tied up at Bayonne, its seagoing days were ended. Increasing numbers of crew were transferred off the ship or discharged. In May, it entered drydock to begin the process of being laid up into reserve status. Later that year, Stanley Carter, the final plank owner—a crewman who had been aboard the ship since its 1938 commissioning—left the ship. He was asked to speak at a farewell, dinner but was too moved to say anything. On February 17 *Enterprise* was decommissioned.

It remained in the reserve fleet at Bayonne for twelve years. In October 1956, the Navy announced that it would be sold for scrapping, along with three battleships that had steamed alongside it: *North Carolina*, *South Dakota*, and *Washington*.

The *Enterprise* Association made an effort to preserve the ship, hoping to fulfill ideas that had been advanced since Navy Day 1945, but to no avail. Even though Congress passed a resolution to establish the ship as a memorial in Washington, the *Enterprise* Association was given only six months to raise the initial two million dollars to move the ship and prepare it for preservation.

This was one mission that *Enterprise*'s men could not accomplish. On July 1, 1958, *Enterprise* was sold for scrap.

During its Navy Day 1945 visit to New York City, USS *Enterprise* is anchored in the Hudson River. Following its arrival in New York, its crew had painted "ENTERPRISE" in large letters on the center of the hull, below the hangar deck, as an identification aid for attendees at the Navy Day celebration. *Naval History and Heritage Command*

In October 1945, *Enterprise* was equipped with additional berthing facilities for returning GIs under Operation Magic Carpet. Subsequently, the ship made two Magic Carpet round trips to Southampton, England, to transport US servicemen back to the United States. *Enterprise* is viewed from along the starboard side facing aft while docked at Southampton in late 1945. *Lt. Col. Herbert Alan Belin*

USS *Enterprise* is viewed off its starboard stern, facing forward, at a pier at Southampton in late 1945. During one of the carrier's visits to that port, its galley staff served a stand-up Thanksgiving dinner to the troops as they boarded. *Lt. Col. Herbert Alan Belin*

The aft part of the flight deck of the *Enterprise* is viewed from the rear of the island during one of the carrier's Operation Magic Carpet voyages across the Atlantic, in late 1945. The stacked life rafts on the deck were an extra precaution because of the many passengers who were embarked. *Lt. Col. Herbert Alan Belin*

In the foreground, servicemen are standing in a boat next to the outer end of Pier 13, Staten Island, with the stern of the *Enterprise* in the background. Returning GIs are crowded onto the fantail of the carrier. *Lt. Col. Herbert Alan Belin*

USS *Enterprise* is docked at Pier 13, Staten Island, New York, on Christmas Eve 1945, following the second of its two round trips to Southampton, England, to bring US servicemen home under Operation Magic Carpet. The bluffs of the community of Stapleton are in the background. *Lt. Col. Herbert Alan Belin*

Pier 13, Staten Island, is decorated with V-for-Victory bunting to welcome home returning GIs. Peeking out from the far side of the pier is the stern of the *Enterprise*. In January 1946, the carrier made one more voyage, to the Azores to ferry personnel from two disabled ships to New York. Following that trip, the *Enterprise* was placed in long-term storage at Bayonne, New Jersey. *Lt. Col. Herbert Alan Belin*

A sailor jotting down notes is standing on the port side of the flight deck of the *Enterprise* at Bayonne on October 18, 1948. The illustrious carrier had been decommissioned on February 17, 1947, and was in long-term storage until a decision was made on its fate. *National Park Service*

After spending a dozen years in long-term storage at Bayonne, New Jersey, the *Enterprise* was towed to the Brooklyn Navy Yard, where it remained for a brief period. The carrier is seen here at Brooklyn on the opposite side of a pier from the new carrier USS *Independence* (CVA-62) on June 22, 1958. On July 1 of that year, the *Enterprise* was sold for salvage for $561,333.00 to the Lipsett Corporation. *National Museum of Naval Aviation*

The carrier *Enterprise* is being towed back to Kearny, New Jersey, for scrapping on August 21, 1958. While at Brooklyn Navy Yard, its tripod mast had been dismounted, and it is visible on the flight deck, aft of the island. *Naval History and Heritage Command*

The job of scrapping the *Enterprise* lasted from August 1958 to February 1960. This view of the island from the flight deck was taken in June 1959. The tripod mast is still lying on the flight deck, aft of the island. *National Museum of Naval Aviation*

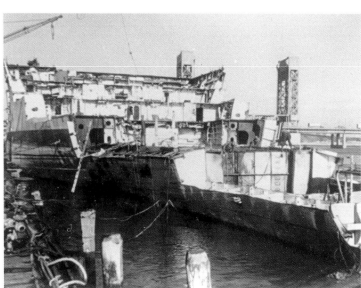

In January 1960, with the scrapping of the *Enterprise* nearing its end, part of the hull is displayed, with several decks visible up to the hangar deck. *National Museum of Naval Aviation*

Workmen are dismantling the bow of the *Enterprise* in January 1960. Draft marks are visible to the right: black above the boot topping, and white on and below the boot topping. *National Museum of Naval Aviation*